The Very, Very Rich & How They Got That Way

AND HOW YOU CAN, TOO!

BY STEVE MARIOTTI
AND MIKE CASLIN
WITH DEBRA DESALVO

PEARSON
Power

An imprint of Pearson Education

This edition is published by arrangement with Pearson Education, Inc. 3 Tice Road, Franklin Lakes NJ 07417, USA and Dorling Kindersley Ltd., 80 Strand, London WC2R ORL UK

PEARSON Power

INDIAN SUBCONTINENT edition published by Dorling Kindersley (India) Pvt. Ltd. (under license from Dorling Kindersley UK) publishing as Pearson Power

ISBN 81-7758-628-9

First Indian Reprint, 2006

This edition is manufactured in India and is authorized for sale only in India, Bangladesh, Bhutan, Pakistan, Nepal, Sri Lanka and the Maldives.

Exclusively distributed in India by Prakash Book.

Published by Dorling Kindersley (India) Pvt. Ltd., licensees of Pearson Education in South Asia.

Head Office: 482, F.I.E., Patparganj, Delhi 110 092, India.
Registered Office: 14 Local Shopping Centre, Panchsheel Park, New Delhi 110 017, India.

Printed in India by Saurabh Printers Pvt. Ltd.

Table of Contents

PART 1: TWENTY AMAZING ENTREPRENEURS

Table of Contents

PART 2: START YOUR OWN BUSINESS

APPENDICES

Introduction

BY STEVE MARIOTTI, PRESIDENT AND FOUNDER OF THE NATIONAL FOUNDATION FOR TEACHING ENTREPRENEURSHIP, INC.

The title to this book is a bit misleading—because most great entrepreneurs have not been motivated by a desire for wealth, but by a vision that they felt compelled to make real. Henry Ford envisioned an automobile in every driveway at a time when cars were considered luxury trifles for the idle rich. Steve Jobs and Stephan Wozniak imagined user-friendly little computers sitting on desks in offices and even in homes at a time when computers were huge cumbersome machines available primarily to academics, the military, and research scientists.

The entrepreneurs profiled in this book did all become very very rich—but each one of them has said that a desire for money, alone, would not have been sufficient motivation for them to have overcome the obstacles they faced. The most successful entrepreneurs have turned out to be those who were highly motivated to create businesses that they believed would improve people's lives. Perhaps that's why entrepreneurs wind up being some of the greatest philanthropists this country has known.

I became fascinated with the stories of America's great entrepreneurs in my late twenties, when I read the biography of William Durant, who founded General Motors in Flint, Michigan. I went to high school in Flint, so I was very aware that Durant had built GM into a world leader in the automobile industry and had opened Flint's first supermarket and bowling alley. What I didn't know, until I read his biography, was that despite becoming one of the richest men in the world, Durant died broke because he committed his wealth to protecting the people of Flint from a collapse in GM's stock price. He spent the last ten years of his life managing the local bowling alley.

I was so amazed by the drama of Durant's life that I began to read ever biography and autobiography of an entrepreneur that I could find—from Ray Kroc, who was economic failure until age 57, to Wozniak and Jobs, who were overnight successes in their early 20s; from Bill Gates, who began his career in entrepreneurship as a 19-year-old Harvard student, to Madame C J. Walker, who was a cleaning lady until age 43 and became the first self-made woman millionaire in America. During one six-week period, I spent every day at the New York Public Library, from 8 a.m. to 8 p.m., reading about entrepreneurs and writing my own little profiles of them, which I found use for when I began to teach entrepreneurship courses in the New York City public school system in the early 1980s. Although I had an MBA from the University of Michigan's School of Business and had had a successful career as a financial analyst for Ford Motor Company, as the owner of a small business, I had come to believe that teaching—especially teaching entrepreneurship to at-risk youth—was my real vocation.

In 1987 I founded the National Foundation for Teaching Entrepreneurship, Inc., which teaches entrepreneurship to thousands of young people worldwide and is leading a national movement in this country to have entrepreneurship education added to the public school curriculum. In fact, eighteen of the nation's top twenty-five young entrepreneurs, as selected by the National Coaltion For Empowering Youth Entrepreneurs in 1998, were NFTE graduates.

Part 2 of this book shows you how to finance your own business ideas and guides you step by step through the same workbook our students have used to write business plans they have used to launch successful businesses. I hope that after reading the stories of America's greatest entrepreneurs, you will be inspired to do the same.

Jeff Bezos

AMAZON.COM

Amazon.com founder Jeff Bezos may be one of the wealthiest people in the world, but he prides himself not on his business acumen but on "being goofy." He said this to Oprah Winfrey during a televised interview in November 1999, in which he also revealed that he had actually wanted to name Amazon.com "Abracadabra" (the idea being to come up with a name that began with "A" so search engines would list it first) but that his lawyer had nixed the idea because he mistakenly thought Bezos wanted to name the business "Cadaver."

"Work **hard**, have **fun**, **make history**."

With his nerdy persona and frequent bursts of loud, infectious laughter, Bezos does seem a bit goofy—and definitely in love with life...and computers. "I've always been a super-nerd," he told Winfrey, "but I'm really super-passionate about computers and how they can make life better." Underneath the laughter and silliness, however, is a very sharp mind, honed on Wall Street, where from 1990 to 1994 he helped design a very technically advanced quantitative hedge fund for D.E. Shaw & Co. Before that, Bezos, who graduated with degrees in electrical engineering and computer science from Princeton in 1986, helped develop computer systems that managed over $250 billion in assets for Bankers Trust. He became Bankers Trust's youngest vice president in 1990.

According to his mother, Jacklyn Gise Bezos, Jeff Bezos always had both intelligence and drive. She told People magazine that by age 3, he demanded to be moved from his crib to a bed. When his mother said No, because she didn't think he was old enough for a bed, Bezos took a screwdriver to his crib to try to turn it into a bed. Recognizing both his precociousness and his drive, Bezos' parents enrolled him in a Montessori preschool, where, his mother recalled, he would sometimes become so engrossed in a project that his teachers had to literally pick him up by the chair and move him in order to get him to focus on something new.

Bezos' grandfather, a retired energy commission manager, was an important influence on his gifted grandson. His grandfather encouraged his interests in science and engineering and Bezos filled his family's garage with science projects. He spent summers on his grandfather's ranch in Cotulla, TX, where he learned to use an arc welder, fix windmills, and castrate cattle. Jeff's father, Miguel Bezos, was an Exxon Corp. executive who had left Cuba in the early 1960s. Like many self-exiled Cubans, Miguel Bezos settled his family—Jacklyn, Jeff, and Jeff's younger brother, Mark, and younger sister, Christine—in Miami. Jeff was class president and valedictorian at Palmetto High School in Miami, where he created the DREAM Institute, a summer program to encourage creative thinking in younger kids.

It makes sense that someone who showed such creativity and wide-ranging interests as a child might get a little bored on Wall Street. Still, it was there that Bezos saw firsthand how computers were revolutionizing the financial services industry. He began to wonder if there was another industry that could be revolutionized by computers, as well. While on Wall Street, he saw statistics indicating that the Internet was growing at a rate of some 2300% per year. This sounded like a revolution to Bezos, who wanted to leave Wall Street and become his own boss.

His strategy was simple: He made a list of twenty products that could be sold online and picked one to

sell. Books won out because Bezos realized he could offer an infinite selection while dodging the cost of opening stores. Bezos decided to move to Seattle because it was close to two major book wholesalers and was home to lots of talented computer whizzes. While driving cross-country with his wife, Mackenzie, Bezos tapped out a business plan on a laptop. They settled into a rented suburban house and set up shop in the garage. It took a year to develop database programs and build the Web site, but by July 1995, Amazon.com was up and running. So were the Bezoses, who were stunned by the number of orders they received.

Today Amazon.com is the third-largest bookseller in the world—the site sells over 57,000 books a day and revenues are expected to top $600 million for 1999. Roughly 13 million people in over 160 countries buy books and other items. In addition to books, the Web site now sells electronics, toys, CDs, videos, and games, and offers free electronic greeting cards and online auctions. Amazon.com hosts a family of Web sites now, including the Internet Movie Database, a comprehensive source of information on over 150,000 movies, LiveBid.com, the sole provider of live-event auctions online, and PlanetAll.com, a Web-based address book, calendar and reminder service.

Despite the business's skyrocketing sales, it has yet to turn a profit, because Bezos has consistently plowed cash back into marketing and acquisitions. Amazon.com has invested heavily in other leading Internet retailers, such as drugstore.com, HomeGrocer.com, and Pets.com. Bezos has been accused of trying to be all things to all shoppers, but his stockholders don't seem to mind. The more money the company lost, the higher its stock climbed, feeding $1.75 billion in capital to Amazon.com from 1997 to late 1999—money Bezos used to keep expanding (Wall Street Journal, "Over The Rainbow With Amazon.com" by Gretchen Morgenson, Nov. 28, 1999). Bezos has a 45% stake in his company, bringing his estimated net worth to $2 billion.

Bezos openly admits that his company will not be profitable until 2002; he points instead to growing repeat orders as an indication that Amazon.com is developing brand loyalty that will result in sustainable profitability. His latest venture is the zShops program, which will enable even very small online retailers to join the Amazon.com family. For $10 a month and a small cut of the sales, Amazon.com will handle customer service for the retailers—from delivery to guarantees. This will put Amazon.com in direct competition with both America Online, which offers an online shopping mall, and Wal-Mart, which is beginning a huge online push. Bezos doesn't care. After all, he already weathered

Barnes & Noble's online entry and dire predictions by Barnes & Noble's head honcho, Forrester Research, that he would turn Amazon.com into "Amazon.toast." Research had to eat his words when Amazon.com's 31% growth in revenue for the first quarter of 1998 beat the pants off Barnes & Noble's 14% growth.

As for the Wal-Mart threat, Bezos told Forbes in the November 1999 issue: "At this point, we have more experience than anyone else in online shopping." The company's mission remains simple, according to Bezos, who told Earthlink's *bLink* magazine (Dec. 1999-Jan. 2000 issue), "The single most important thing is to focus obsessively on the customer....Our goal is to be Earth's most customer-centric company."

MORE ABOUT JEFF BEZOS

Company Web Site: www.amazon.com

Business The Amazon.Com Way: Secrets Of the World's Most Amazing Web Business
by Rebecca Saunders (Capstone Ltd., 1999)

Richard Branson

VIRGIN GROUP LTD.

Adventurous, brash, and brilliant are just some of the adjectives used to describe British entrepreneur Richard Branson, as well as his mega-company, Virgin Group Ltd. "Capitalist hippie" is another label applied to Branson, who usually sports longish hair, a goatee, and blue jeans. But the strangest may be "billionaire balloonist."

"One night in jail teaches you that ***sleeping well*** *at night is the only thing that really matters."*

Branson has attempted to become the first balloonist to circle the globe four times. He was the first to cross both the Atlantic and Pacific oceans by balloon, but his most recent attempt to circumnavigate the world failed when bad weather forced him and his team to ditch their balloon in the Pacific Ocean on Christmas Day, 1998. When his rivals, balloonists Brian Jones and Bertrand Piccard, were about to reach their goal almost a year later, Branson congratulated them on their achievement, while joking that he was ordering Virgin Atlantic airplanes to "intercept the balloon before it reaches its end." [Associated Press, Mar. 19, 1999]

BRANSON STARTED HIS FIRST BUSINESS AT AGE 16

Branson may have gotten his aviation gene from his mother, who was a glider pilot and a flight attendant before she married his father, who was a lawyer. Branson was born in 1950 in a London suburb. His parents always encouraged him to never just stand by and watch other people do things.

Branson is dyslexic, however, so school was very difficult for him. Frustrated by school and inspired by the student activist movement of the late 1960s, Branson decided to start his own student newspaper, called, appropriately enough, Student. His unique angle was to market the paper not just to students at his exclusive English boarding school, Stowe, but to students at many different schools. Branson wanted to create an "alternative culture" magazine that would bring together other students his age.

Branson wrote a business plan with his friend Jonny Gems and Branson's mother donated four pounds ($6.00) to cover stamp and phone costs. Gems and Branson had big ideas. They planned to sell ads to corporations and have articles by rock and film stars, intellectuals, and politicians. For the first issue they scored a cover drawn by Peter Blake, who designed the Beatles' *Sgt. Pepper's Lonely Hearts Club Band* album cover. Branson sold $10,000 in advertising for the first issue of his magazine and persuaded such star writers as Jean-Paul Sartre and John Le Carré to write articles. The first issue sold around 50,000 copies, so Branson quit school to run the magazine. Stowe's headmaster wrote Branson a note: "Congratulations, Branson. I predict that you will either go to prison or become a millionaire." [*Richard Branson: The Authorized Biography* by Mick Brown]

The magazine started losing money a few years later, but by then Branson had noticed a new opportunity to start a business that would appeal to the same market he already knew quite well. In 1970 the British government abolished a law that kept retail record prices at a certain level, but none of the record stores dropped their prices. Branson decided to sell discounted records to students. Because he did not have the overhead of a record store, Branson decided to make his company, Virgin Records, mail-order. Branson chose the name Virgin to reflect his business inexperience.

Orders poured in, but his success was interrupted by a postal strike the following year. Since he couldn't sell his discounted records through the mail, Branson opened Britain's first discount record store. He also bought a recording studio. The young entrepreneur soon found himself strapped for cash, though. To cover his bills he sold tax-exempt export records domestically. This was illegal and Branson actually spent a night in jail on tax fraud charges. His parents had to mortgage their home to cover his bail. Branson pled guilty and had to pay $85,000 in fines. The experience taught him, he has said, that no profit is worth the worry of being caught doing something illegal.

VIRGIN'S FIRST RECORD SELLS 7 MILLION COPIES

In 1973, Branson's cousin Simon Draper became his partner. Together, they produced Virgin's first original recording. The record, an instrumental album by Mike Oldfield called Tubular Bells, was a huge hit. It sold more than 7 million copies and was used on the soundtrack of the movie *The Exorcist*.

Branson found that he had an ear for discovering exciting musical talent. He took a huge chance when he signed some punk rockers called the Sex Pistols; another when he signed a cross-dressing white soul singer named Boy George. Both artists became worldwide sensations.

ENTERING THE AIRLINE BUSINESS

Flush with cash, Branson was ready for a new challenge when a California lawyer named Randolph Fields contacted him about financing a new airline that would provide a business-class route between London and New York. Branson's advisers were against the deal. They were fearful of getting into a bruising competition with British Airways, which virtually monopolized commercial flights out of London's Heathrow Airport.

Branson decided to go into the airline business, however, because he realized how close to the entertainment business it really was. His strategy was to offer first-class services to customers flying business class. Most business flyers were used to low fares, cramped seats, terrible food, and a long, dull flight. For about half the price of British Airways' first-class service, Virgin offered a special business class called Upper Class that treated business travelers to sleeper seats, stand-up lounges, free neck massages and manicures, a seat-back video screen for each passenger, and fine food and wine. Upper Class service was so profitable and successful that it gave Branson room to offer economy fares, as well, that appealed to his old market—poor but travel-happy students.

DAREDEVIL STUNTS FOR PUBLICITY

Years promoting artists like the Sex Pistols and Boy George had given Branson an appreciation for the attention-getting appeal of outrageousness. To gain attention for Virgin Atlantic Airways and distance it from British Airways' stiff image, he staged daredevil stunts guaranteed to attract media coverage. He made two attempts to break the transatlantic speed record for powerboats. The first time, he crashed and sank, but the second time he made the world record.

With Swedish balloonist Per Linstrand, Branson became the first person to cross the Atlantic in a hot-air balloon. He and Linstrand tried in 1991 to cross from Japan to California in a balloon and were stranded in arctic Canada for six hours. Their adventures provided millions of dollars worth of free publicity for Virgin, as well as an attractive image as a hip, fun company.

British Airways was hit hard by Virgin's success and soon the two companies were wrangling in court. Branson argued that British Airways was waging a "dirty tricks campaign" against Virgin by flooding the market with discount tickets and sneaking into Virgin's computer system to steal Upper Class customers. He even filed a libel suit, accusing British Airways of hiring private detectives to dig up dirt about him.

British Airways was eventually ordered to pay Virgin Atlantic nearly $1 million in damages. But Branson wasn't satisfied. He wanted to break what he perceived as British Airways' control of Heathrow Airport and ongoing unfair pricing and business practices.

BRANSON SELLS HIS MUSIC COMPANY TO FIGHT HIS AIRLINE BATTLE

To fight his battle, Branson sold Virgin Music Group to Thorn EMI in 1992 for $900 million in cash. He personally pocketed $515 million from the deal. He gained hundreds of millions more from the sale of his majority control of the Virgin record retail stores and his computer games business.

These sales armed him with $700 million to compete with British Airways. "British Airways has spent the last two years trying to push us into the abyss," Branson told Vanity Fair magazine, "Now it's time for them to accept that there'll be two British airlines for the next fifty years."

Branson proved it by adding new routes from London to San Francisco, Chicago, and Johannesburg, South Africa. By early 1999 his airline had grown so much that it was Virgin, not British Airways, to which the British Civil Aviation Authority granted the coveted right to develop a direct flight between London and Shanghai.

BRANSON'S UNIQUE MANAGEMENT STYLE

Interestingly, Branson chose to share much of his settlement from British Airways with Virgin Atlantic employees. Each employee received roughly $400. Branson believes strongly in trying to keep his employees happy and committed to the company. About twenty of his managing directors and presidents have become millionaires. Branson also believes in challenging his employees. He told *Success* magazine, "When people are put into positions slightly above what they would expect, they're apt to excel." He keeps each of his companies small, because he believes everyone should know everyone else in a particular company.

Branson's conglomerate, The Virgin Group, employs over 7500 people worldwide. He encourages employees to call him by his first name and contact him directly with any concerns. His casual style — he favors blue jeans and sweaters over suits and ties — is in keeping with the relaxed, creative environment he seeks to maintain at his companies.

In the 1990s Branson has expanded primarily by creating joint ventures and outside partnerships. He wisely entered into partnerships with several Japanese companies that not only supplied Virgin with capital but also helped introduce the company to profitable Japanese markets. He took advantage of Virgin's hip image by licensing the company's name for use on a wide range of products, from personal computers to vodka and cola.

If the performance of his cola business is any indication, this licensing approach could be a huge success. Within a month of going on sale in Britain, Virgin Cola, which was priced 25% below Coke and Pepsi, captured 15% of the British cola market. "We're already earning a million pounds a week in profit," Branson said at the time. He predicts that the cola business could be worth a half billion dollars within a couple of years.

TACKLING AOL

Branson's latest venture is Virgin Net. He announced in October 1999 that he was planning to spend 50 million pounds ($75 million) to involve virtually every aspect of his company in electronic commerce. His first move was to offer free Internet access to subscribers to Virgin Net. This was a direct slap at America Online, which is Britain's dominate Interest service provider (ISP) and charges its customers a monthly fee. Branson's Web plans include not only Virgin Net but Virgin Atlantic, which will sell tickets online; an online Virgin Megastore that will offer 60,000 more CDs than Amazon.com;

online booking for Virgin Trains; live music Webcasts from V2 Music; Virgin Direct, which will allow customers to handle their finances online; and Virgin Bride, an online wedding planning site.

Most entrepreneurs would avoid tangling with powerful competitors like British Airways, AOL, and Coke, but Branson seems to relish the challenge. "What does the Virgin name mean?" he asked himself in a 1997 interview with Forbes. "We're a company that likes to take on the giants. In too many businesses these giants have had things their own way. We're going to have a lot of fun competing with them."

FOR MORE ABOUT RICHARD BRANSON

Company Web Site: www.virgin.com

Losing My Virginity by Richard Branson

Richard Branson, Virgin King: Inside Richard Branson's Business Empire by Tim Jackson

Richard Branson: The Authorized Biography by Mick Brown

Thomas J. Burrell

BURRELL COMMUNICATIONS GROUP: ADVERTISING TO AFRICAN AMERICANS

Chicago native Thomas Burrell founded the first black-owned advertising agency in 1971. After six months in business he was penniless, but by 1972 he had landed a huge client—McDonald's. His campaign for McDonald's was one of the first to target a specific ethnic or racial demographic, and it was very successful. Soon other household names were clamoring for Burrell to create campaigns for them.

"The important thing is to enjoy yourself and continue to work. I know life is a journey, not a destination. That's also true in business — your objectives keep moving."

By specializing in campaigns geared toward African-American audiences, Burrell grew his agency into a multi-million-dollar major player in advertising. In 1998, Burrell Communications Group billed $168 million. Today his clients include McDonald's, Coca-Cola, Kraft Foods, Mobil, Procter & Gamble, and Sears. Burrell was even hired by the Democratic Party to target ads to African-American voters during 1996, and black male voter turnout skyrocketed as a result. In October, 1999, Burrell was tapped by Vice President Al Gore to co-create a permanent task force to promote multicultural advertising. [*Black Journalism Review*, Oct. 24, 1999] This represents an unprecedented level of success for an African-American entrepreneur in advertising.

A HIGH SCHOOL APTITUDE TEST ENCOURAGES BURRELL TO TRY ADVERTISING

Born on March 18, 1939, Burrell was raised by his mother, a beautician, in a tough area of Chicago's South Side. In high school, he took an aptitude test that had a dramatic impact on his life. He scored poorly, except in two areas: artistic ability and persuasive ability. Unsure how to interpret these results, he asked his teacher what it meant. She suggested that he consider a career writing advertising copy. With this new sense of direction, Burrell's schoolwork improved. He was accepted at Chicago's Roosevelt University, where he studied advertising and English. He figured that having a solid command of English was essential to pursuing a career in advertising. In 1961, he received his B.A. in English.

While in college, Burrell got his first job connected with advertising. In 1960, a friend told him that Wade Advertising Agency was open to the idea of hiring a young African-American to work in their mailroom. Burrell got the mailroom job at $50 a week. Even though it was a menial job, he was the only African-American, at that time, working for a major Chicago advertising agency.

BURRELL MOVES UP FROM THE MAILROOM

"From the moment I got there," Burrell recalled, "I went on a rampage trying to move into the copywriting area. One of the great things about working in the mailroom is you get a chance to see what's going on in the company. So I assigned myself a project. Then one day I was rolling my wagon by the creative director's office and saw he was not busy." Burrell walked right into the creative director's office and boldly told him he would be of far greater benefit to the company if he could use his abilities to solve "critical problems." At that point, he took out some sample ads he had prepared. The creative director was so impressed that, within a week, Burrell was promoted to the job of copywriter trainee. Within three months, he was promoted to the level of copywriter. He was creating television and print campaigns for such accounts as Alka-Seltzer, One-a-Day Vitamins, and Falstaff beer. Sheer assertiveness and working hard at what he really enjoyed had carried him far in only a short time.

Burrell's next job was with a bigger advertising company, Leo Burnett (also in Chicago), and it involved bigger clients. Burrell's copywriting skills improved rapidly as he worked on such major "package-goods" accounts as Pillsbury, Swanson Frozen Foods, and Vick Chemical. After three years with Burnett, he went overseas to work in London on the British Overseas Airways account.

In 1968, he returned to the U.S. and became Copy Supervisor at Needham, Harper and Steers. While there, he developed major new advertising campaigns for General Mills and Schick. By now Burrell had mastered copywriting. He was determined to open his own advertising agency.

BURRELL CONVINCES MCDONALD'S HE CAN EXPAND ITS AFRICAN-AMERICAN MARKET

In 1971, with an art director Burrell had met at Needham, he started his own company — Burrell McBain Advertising. It was a struggle, however, and six months later Burrell was broke. But he persevered and in 1972 he landed a big fish — McDonald's. Burrell had successfully convinced McDonald's management that he could help them make inroads into the African-American market, which was largely ignored by advertising. Since then, Burrell Advertising has created over a hundred commercials for McDonald's, which is Burrell's biggest client. Other major clients are Coca-Cola, Ford Motor, Johnson Products, Joseph Schlitz Brewing, Blockbuster Entertainment, Proctor & Gamble, Jack Daniel Distillery, Polaroid, Stroh Brewing, and First National Bank of Chicago.

Burrell believes that commercials are most successful if they can reflect consumers' values back to them in ways that strike an emotional chord. He calls this using "emotional envelopes" to deliver key messages about the client's product.

"POSITIVE REALISM"

Burrell called his advertising philosophy "positive realism." As he explained it: "I found that if you give the consumer a snapshot where he could see himself as he really is and the way he wants to be portrayed, people really respond to it. That emotionalism translates into behavior in the marketplace."

He elaborated: "We wanted to make sure the consumer understood the advertiser was inviting that consumer — that black consumer — to participate as a consumer of their product. Black consumers have not felt they were being extended an invitation." One commercial for McDonald's was set at a black family reunion, for instance. Another series emphasized the importance of the father in keeping black families together.

Burrell's unique approach has not gone unnoticed by the advertising industry. For a Coca-Cola TV ad and for the McDonald's family reunion commercial, Burrell won Clio Awards. The Clio is the advertising industry's highest award, equivalent in prestige to the Oscars for the motion picture industry. The Chicago advertising community honored Burrell as "Advertising Person of the Year" for 1985-86, with the prestigious Albert Lasker Award for lifetime achievement in advertising.

BURRELL STARTS PUBLIC RELATIONS AND CONSUMER PROMOTIONS COMPANIES

In 1988, Burrell extended the entrepreneurial success of Burrell Advertising by founding two related companies: Burrell Public Relations Inc. and Burrell Consumer Promotions Inc. In 1995 Burrell acquired DFA Advertising to boost its creative side and aid in its expansion into advertising targeted not just at African Americans but at Hispanics and Asians, as well.

RACISM ENCOURAGED BURRELL TO BECOME AN ENTREPRENEUR

Burrell has spoken candidly of two important influences on his career. One was his mother, who, from the time he was a child, encouraged him to think for himself and be self-reliant. The other was his African-American heritage. It is not surprising that a powerful statue of Martin Luther King stands in the waiting room of his office.

Burrell has said that racism actually encouraged him to become an entrepreneur: "I felt that no matter how successful I might have been at that time [in the late 1960s] there was a ceiling that would certainly prevent me from going all the way in someone else's company. And even if I could go all the way it would still not be my company."

"It's an unfortunate thing that being a black-owned company means, for some people, that you should be limited to addressing blacks only," Burrell added. "If there are ninety-nine bigots out there who say we won't do business with a black I'm looking for that hundredth person who will. I've got to believe that who owns an ad agency will at some point become irrelevant. What will matter will be the kind of advertising the agency does, how capable the agency is."

Nonetheless, Burrell is a realist who empathizes with minorities who feel overwhelmed by the obstacles of racial prejudice. He advised those who feel this to first admit that these obstacles exist and then ask: "Now what do I do?" He warned that if you don't try, "You are definitely going to lose. You can't be afraid to fail. "Smiling, he added, "I've been a black person all my life and I will be for the rest of my life. The only thing I know how to do is stay positive. You stay positive and something good will happen."

Burrell says the Internet gives African Americans the best shot they've had yet at participating in business. "It's going to be used the same way traditional media is," he told *The Industry Standard* (October 24, 1999), but "you can get into it without having to deal with the race thing."

"TO BE THE BEST TOM BURRELL THAT I CAN BE"

Still fit and imposing at age 60, the 6'4" Burrell describes his personal philosophy simply: "To be the best Tom Burrell that I can be." In reflecting on life and work, Burrell said: "The important thing is to enjoy yourself and continue to work. I know life is a journey, not a destination.

"That's also true in business — your objectives keep moving. When I started this business, I said if we could become a $5 million agency that would be terrific." He believes that "You grow a business by picking the best people you can find, giving them responsibility and accountability."

Practicing what he preaches, Burrell appointed a new president and chief operating officer for Burrell Communications Group while remaining chairman and chief executive. This freed him to focus more of his energies on his work for Vice President Gore's commission and his many business and community affiliations. Burrell is a member of the boards of directors of the Chicago Urban League, the Citizenship Education Fund, of the board of governors of the Chicago Lighthouse for the Blind, Co-Chair of the Minority Business Development Task Force for Chicago United, a member of the Chicago Urban League's Business Advisory Council, and a member of the President's Advisory Council of Roosevelt University. He is also a member of the Advisory Council of Howard University's School of Communications.

Despite his deep dedication to his demanding business and social enterprises, Burrell manages to lead a well-rounded life. He is married and has three children. He is a music and art lover, and collects outstanding examples of African-American art, which richly decorate both his office and home. Making people aware of African-American contributions to the arts is very

important to him. He also loves traveling, and considers it vital to keep in good physical condition.

Today, Burrell Communications Group is always first or second on the short list of companies seeking to target the African-American market. Burrell understands that minorities now make up one in four Americans and that this proportion is expected to rise to one in three by 2005 (*Afrocentric News*, October 1999). He plans to make sure they feel represented in the mirror world of our society we call advertising.

Candice Carpenter

iVILLAGE

iVillage.com

In 1995 Candice Carpenter was a 43-year-old single working mom who didn't even own a computer. She was a respected executive, however, who had successfully run Q2, Barry Diller's high-end home-shopping channel. Prior to that she was president of Time-Life Video and Television, where she developed prime time documentary miniseries for NBC, CBS and syndication, including Rolling Stone History of Rock and Roll and Lost Civilizations.

"**Success** is about creating **value**."

When Carpenter finally did buy a personal computer so she could do some consulting for AOL, she never imagined she'd start her own Web site—and that the site, iVillage, would soon become the number one destination for women on the Web.

AOL hired Carpenter to help figure out how AOL could create content that would draw the customers its advertisers wanted to see. Before 1995, AOL made most of its money by charging customers hourly access fees. Once competing Internet service providers (ISPs) like Earthlink began offering flat-rate access, however, AOL had to offer it, also, and try to fill the hole in its revenue with advertising fees.

According to David Carnoy's profile of Carpenter in *Success* (January 1999), she told AOL executives that what they really needed to do was develop branded companies under the AOL umbrella that would build consumer followings. She had noticed that there were a few Web sites that were geared toward consumers with unique interests, such as technology or sports, but nothing for people with more general interests. She recommended that AOL hire some experienced managers to create such sites. AOL responded by suggesting that she set up her own company and create the sites herself. Which just goes to show that if you have a business idea, your employer may actually become your partner!

Armed with a $2 million stake from AOL, in exchange for 20 percent of her company, Carpenter decided to focus on baby boomers, an affluent group that was signing on to AOL in droves. She and her co-partners, Nancy Evans and Robert Levitan, launched three sites, on parenting, health and careers—baby boomers' top priorities.

But the boomers turned out to be the sites' focus only for the first year. Carpenter quickly discovered that 80 percent of the audience was women. Several advertisers even encouraged her to focus on women. Carpenter did a little digging and discovered that, as she told *New Media* magazine ("Compelling Content for Wired Women, by Gillina Newson, April 14, 1998), "More than 8 million businesses are women-owned; 62 percent of the new investors on Wall Street are women; 25 percent of women in dual-income relationships are bringing home the bigger paycheck." Carpenter decided to re-tool, and iVillage: The Women's Network was born, designed to focus on "women who have no time."

Women like Carpenter, in other words, who is definitely not the type to lounge around reading fashion magazines. Carpenter holds an MBA from Harvard and serves on the board of directors of the Breakthrough Foundation, an organization that provides opportunities for inner-city children. She's not afraid of challenges, in fact, she embraces them. "My character was formed by mountaineering," she told Anna Muoio for a *Fast Company* magazine profile (June 1997), "Enduring rainy slopes and cold bivouacs to spend an hour at the top of the world shaped my ability to handle adversity.

If you are committed to creating value, and if you aren't afraid of the hard times, obstacles become utterly unimportant. A nuisance, perhaps, but with no real power. The world respects creation. People will get out of your way."

Her first challenge was to raise enough money to make the site a major Internet player, and this she accomplished by wooing investors relentlessly. "We were obsessively focused not only in getting investors, but in choosing those who would facilitate us in implementing our vision," she told *MoneyHunter*. To AOL's stake she was able to add venture capital from TCI Interactive and Tribune. By 1998 she had also formed strategic partnerships with NBC, which took an equity stake in the company and provided on-air promotion and distribution of iVillage content on Snap.com.

That Carpenter was able to bring such high-powered investors on board is proof of her tenacity. She attributes it, in part, to what she calls "radical mentors," senior executives she has encountered during her career who have pushed her beyond her limits. As she told *Fast Company's* Katharine Mieszkowski ("Radical Mentoring," issue 17), "People don't grow if you're soft with them. You catapult people forward by being extremely blunt." Carpenter doesn't hesitate to radically mentor members of her own staff in the same way, provided they want it. "I can do this with only a few people at a time," she notes. "It takes a lot of energy."

Carpenter can be intimidating but she's also insightful and sensitive. Years of Alcoholics Anonymous meetings and teaching Outward Bound programs have given her a strong belief in the power of community. As she learned more about the Internet, she began to believe that iVillage could provide an online community for women. "The principle of iVillage is essentially humanizing cyber-space by creating communities where people can interact on a common subject," she told MoneyHunter Mentors.

To do that Carpenter sought sponsorships from advertisers who she felt would resonate with her target audience and allowed them to not just place banner ads, but to create sites within iVillage from which they could directly address consumers. Her unusual approach brought major advertisers like Starbucks, FedEx, Toyota, and Visa aboard. Advertising provides iVillage with about 90 percent of its revenue, although Carpenter hopes that within the next three years it will decline to 60 percent as merchandising and premium usage fees add to iVillage coffers. She encourages her advertisers to let her audience know that they have "empathy for what women are going through."

She also encouraged users of the site to help generate the content. Three hundred volunteers host chats and encourage interaction. Communities have formed spontaneously on iVillage as a result. According to the *New Media* article "Compelling Content for Wired Women," (April 14, 1998), a group called The Management Community formed when a group of parents agreed to try not criticizing their teenagers for one week. These parents, and others, formed the community to share their experiences and suggestions for dealing with their kids.

This is exactly how Carpenter had hoped the site would work—to provide women with quick access to information and advice they can use to run their families and their careers more efficiently. As Carpenter told *MoneyHunter*, "For example, I'm a single parent, and I'm making a foreign adoption. My next-door neighbor is unlikely to be helpful on these specific issues, but if I go online, I can talk to people all over the world who are doing the same thing and are, in essence, parenting experts."

The catch is that iVillage has advertisers and revenue but no profit—yet. Women clearly like the content—the site's monthly number of visitors has doubled from 3 million in 1998 to 6 million. But the company reported losses of $43.7 million in 1998. Nonetheless Carpenter was able to raise over $80 million in an IPO offering in March. Carpenter used that capital to acquire a stake in iBaby, which sells 20,000 infant products online, as part of her effort to encourage women to not just visit iVillage, but to shop there, as well. She's certainly up to the challenge of turning iVillage into a profitable business. As she told Mieszkowski, "Once you get your first taste of being really challenged, you want to be challenged more."

FOR MORE ON CARPENTER

Company Web site: www.ivillage.com

Debbi Fields

MRS. FIELDS' ORIGINAL COOKIES INC.: GOOD ENOUGH NEVER IS

Debbi Fields opened her first cookie store when she was only nineteen. She had been baking chocolate-chip cookies that everyone loved since she was thirteen, but she knew nothing about running a store. By the time she was thirty, though, she owned more than five hundred Mrs. Fields' Cookies stores in over twenty-five states and five foreign countries. Today her company, Mrs. Fields' Original Cookies Inc., grosses over $300 million annually from over 1000 outlets in nine countries.

*"Once you find something you **love** to do, be the **best** at doing it."*

More than anything, Fields' credits her positive attitude for her huge success despite the odds faced by a young housewife starting her very first small business. Fields developed that attitude while growing up in a tough section of East Oakland, California, in a small house with her three sisters, her mom, and her dad. Her father repaired machine parts at a U.S. navy base. There wasn't much money, but the family was happy. Field's father always said that his wealth wasn't in money but in the love of his family and friends. That idea guided Fields when she started her own business. Later, when people would ask her how to make a million dollars, she would tell them: "If you chase money, you'll never catch it," and would advise them to do something they loved.

Debbi was the youngest of the four Fields girls, so she was always tagging along after her big sisters, trying to get them to pay some attention to her. She always felt sort of dumb, because her sisters were bigger and smarter than she was, but she also held onto a secret belief that she was somebody special.

Being smart didn't seem to really matter, anyway, because she was a girl. When she was growing up in the late 1950s girls were told that they didn't have to be smart, they just had to learn how to keep house so they could take good care of a husband and kids someday.

Fields coasted through school, feeling vaguely bored and unhappy. She had this urge to be somebody, but didn't have any idea what to do with it. By the time she was thirteen, she also realized that she was tired of wearing her sisters' old clothes. She wanted some things of her own.

WORKING GIVES FIELDS CONFIDENCE

Her solution was to get a job as a foul-line ball girl for the Oakland A's baseball team. She loved chasing down foul balls in the Alameda County Stadium in front of a huge crowd, and getting to know the baseball players, but most of all she loved working. As she wrote in her autobiography, *One Smart Cookie*, "finding out I could compete in the workplace gave me a much better feeling about myself than I'd ever had before." She lost any trace of shyness and learned how to handle herself in the public eye, which would be helpful later when she became a well-known businesswoman.

She also noticed that some of the baseball players were very kind to the kids who asked for their autographs after the game, while other players were cold and rude. She saw the hurt on the faces of the kids who had been snubbed by a player who thought he was too important to talk to them.

"I didn't know it then, of course, but here was the beginning of Mrs. Fields' Cookies — a thirteen-year-old girl's instinctive understanding that everyone on earth needs to feel important," she wrote in her autobiography.

Fields' next job was at a department store, where she put into practice what she'd noticed in her ball-girl job. She was enthusiastic and friendly to the customers. Her hard work and good attitude was noticed and rewarded by her employer. She had finally found an environment where she could be special.

MARINE WORLD: A LESSON IN THE POWER OF ENTHUSIASM

When she was seventeen she got a job at Marine World as a water skier. She was soon promoted to performing with the dolphins, and got a kick out of the delighted Marine World audiences. Finally, she felt that something was happening in her life, but more importantly, she had learned how to make things happen. Later she would teach the staff at her stores the importance of being enthusiastic — even a bit silly — just to create an air of excitement that would attract customers.

When Fields graduated from high school, she moved to Lake Tahoe to do some skiing and figure out what to do with her life. She supported herself by working as a nanny for a family. After a few months she returned home and became a ski bum, working dead-end retail jobs and spending her money on ski trips to Tahoe or Aspen.

While waiting in an airport in Denver on one ski trip, she met Randy Fields. He was an economist, ten years older than she was, and he called her parents' house every half hour until she finally agreed to go out with him on their first date.

Soon they got married. Randy's reputation as a brilliant economist grew. Being the wife of an older man who was getting a lot of attention for his career made Fields want to accomplish something herself. She'd noticed how much friends loved her chocolate-chip cookies. Here, she thought, was something she could really do. She decided to start a business selling her cookies to the public.

NO ONE SUPPORTED HER BUSINESS IDEA

No one — not her family, not her friends, not even her husband, thought this was a good idea. Her cookies were soft and chewy — not crispy like store brands — and they needed to be eaten fresh to taste their best.

Fields refused to give up on her idea, so her husband decided he owed her his full support, even though he thought it would never work. They finally secured a loan through a banker they already knew, as he had given them the mortgage on their home. He, too, told them it would never work, but he trusted them to at least pay back the loan.

Fields knew two crucial things, though: she knew how to bake and she knew from her earlier job experiences how to treat customers. She opened her cookie store on August 1, 1977 in Palo Alto, California. Still, the first day she was open, she hadn't sold a single cookie by noon.

GIVING AWAY COOKIES

Trying not to panic, Fields loaded up a tray with cookies and walked around the shopping arcade offering them to shoppers for free. She fought her embarrassment and walked around the stores and the parking lot until a few people began trying the cookies.

Her strategy worked: within an hour customers were at her store buying cookies. She sold fifty dollars' worth that day and seventy-five dollars' worth the next. She was in business, but more importantly, she had found a strategy. To this day the policy at Mrs. Fields' stores is to give customers free samples to encourage them to buy cookies.

About a year later, Fields opened a second store in a shopping mall in San Francisco. To staff her stores she hired people who struck her as warm and friendly. She encouraged them to have fun and be themselves as long as they could bake cookies that were up to her standards.

NO COMPROMISE ON QUALITY

Fields was never willing to compromise the quality of her cookies, even if more profit could be made. She refused to use cheaper margarine-butter blends as a substitute for pure butter, for instance, even though she would have saved a lot of money.

Fields learned all she could about bookkeeping, taxes and accounting. To her surprise she found out she was pretty smart after all. Soon another store opened and all three were flourishing due to Debbi's insistence on three things: a great location for each store, no compromise on cookie quality, and enthusiastic store employees.

Running around trying to keep all three stores up to her standards was exhausting Fields, however. One thing she was not good at was trusting other people to do things properly. This flaw was partly responsible years later for the crisis in the company. For now, though, she thought about selling half the business to a friend. Randy convinced her not to do it.

The business grew rapidly, but most of the profits were going back to pay off bank loans used to open the new stores. By this time both she and Randy were exhausted from running the business, so they tried to sell it to a giant food corporation. The sale didn't go through, and the Fields were forced to go back to the banks for financing.

Again and again they were told that selling cookies was not a "real" business like selling steel or cars. They had to fight for the financing they needed. By the time they finally got the money, the Fieldses realized that they didn't want to sell the business anymore. It meant too much to them.

Nor did they want to expand through franchising. Having worked so hard to establish high quality standards, Fields didn't want to rent her name and reputation to franchisees who would be more interested in profit than quality. To her mind, profit followed from quality. Later she would change her mind and develop a very successful franchise program.

NOT GOOD ENOUGH

One day Fields walked into her third store and noticed that the cookies looked flat and overbaked. When she asked the young man who was selling that day what he thought of the cookies, he told her, "Aw, they're good enough." Fields silently slid each tray of cookies into the garbage — dumping about five or six hundred dollars worth of cookies — and told him: "Good enough never is." That's been the motto of the Mrs. Fields' Cookies company ever since.

By 1984 the Fieldses had three children and over two hundred stores from California to New York. The company had become a leading corporate supporter of the campaign to find a cure for cystic fibrosis, a disease that kills many children. It had also begun to expand internationally by opening stores in Japan, Hong Kong, and Australia.

Fields continued to create new cookie recipes and to modify existing recipes to please customers in different locations. In Hawaii, for instance, people loved the macadamia nut cookies. East Coast stores sold more dark chocolate chip cookies than the West Coast, where customers preferred milk chocolate.

Rather than hire marketing consultants to tell her what kinds of cookies people would want in Japan or Hong Kong, Fields simply went there, opened a store and began giving cookies away, asking customers what they liked and didn't like. She refused to advertise her cookies, believing that the product would speak for itself and that giving cookies away was the best advertising.

HER HUSBAND JOINS THE BUSINESS

In 1986 Randy quit doing economic consulting and joined his wife's business. Although the company was now profitable, bank loans were still needed to open new stores and the Fields were very tired of dealing with bankers. They decided to sell shares in the company to the public and use the cash to pay off the banks and finance further expansion.

They decided to go public on the London Stock Exchange's unlisted securities market first because this was easier and cheaper than selling stock on the American market. The stock was offered in London in the spring of 1986. It did not do well at first because the company was not that well known in Britain, but soon the stock price did improve.

When the stock was offered in the U.S. the following year it did very well. The Fields were operating 543 stores in six countries and the company earned $18 million in profit on sales of $104 million that year.

ALMOST TOO MUCH, TOO FAST

The company was growing like crazy and even bought a bakery chain from PepsiCo. The rapid growth, combined with Fields' unwillingness to let other people take much responsibility, almost caused the business to fall apart in 1988, however. Like most entrepreneurs, Fields was used to doing everything herself. It was difficult for her to trust the daily running of the business to professional managers.

The qualities that make someone a great entrepreneur — creativity, passion, risk-taking — do not necessarily make that person a great business manager. Managers are more down-to-earth and conservative, but that makes them good at taking care of the boring details of running the business. This frees the entrepreneur to be innovative and creative.

Too many new stores had opened too close to existing ones and sales were falling as a result. The stock price fell to new lows. Fields closed 97 stores that year and realized that she would have to find good managers and trust them with helping her and Randy run the business. She hired a chief financial officer from a top accounting firm and a head of operations who had lots of experience in the food business. She made herself let them handle the day-to-day details of running the business.

This left her free to develop new ideas. The name Mrs. Fields meant top-quality baked goods to customers all over the world, so she began thinking up ways to use the name for more than just cookies and brownies. Fields made a deal with Ambrosia Chocolate to make and market Mrs. Fields' semi-sweet chocolate chips, and she began testing recipes for muffins, bread, sandwiches and soup for her new Mrs. Fields' Bakeries.

To compensate for the closed stores, Fields introduced her popular mail order service in 1988. She started small—selling only tins of cookies—but today the mail order division offers a 20-page catalog with a variety of gift packages.

In response, the stock price for Mrs. Fields' Cookies headed back up and the company has been on a roll ever since. Fields overcame her reluctance to franchising and began selling franchises in 1990.

Letting go of the daily details has given Fields more time to read every comment sent to the company by customers and to travel around visiting her stores and meeting with local managers. She opened www.mrsfields.com in 1997 and also developed Mrs. Fields' Franchises. Today her company is considered the nation's leading retailer and franchisor of "baked on premises" products. Fields has further consolidated her share of this market by acquiring Pretzelmaker's 299 stores in November 1998, bringing the total number of stores under her company's umbrella to 1,553—nearly 1,000 of which are licensed or franchised (Franchise News, November 23, 1998).

After 22 years in business, Debbi Fields shows no sign of letting up. But she has learned to let go and to make the most of her talents for innovation and, of course, cookies! Reorganizing her business freed her up to not only spend more time with her five daughters but to write three cookbooks: *I Love Chocolate; The Mrs. Fields' Cookie Book*, which was the first book about cookies to make the New York Times bestseller list; and most recently, *Debbi Fields' Great American Desserts*.

FOR MORE ABOUT DEBBI FIELDS

Company Web Site: www.mrsfields.com

One Smart Cookie by Debbi Fields

Henry Ford

FORD MOTOR COMPANY: AN AUTOMOBILE IN FRONT OF EVERY HOME

Henry Ford's career is one of the most incredible in the history of American business. By the time he was close to forty, he had several failed businesses and was broke. His neighbors considered him a daydreaming mechanic who tinkered with worthless contraptions. By age fifty, though, Ford was one of the richest, most celebrated men in the world. Today Ford Motor Company is the world's largest producer of trucks, the world's second largest producer of cars and trucks combined, and one of the largest providers of financial services worldwide. Not bad for a Michigan farmboy!

"Failure is a chance to begin again more intelligently. It is just a resting place. We learn more from our failures than our successes"

Ford was born on a farm near Dearborn, Michigan, a few miles west of Detroit. The child of middle-class farmers, he was the eldest of six children. When he was only twelve, his beloved mother died. The boy was forced to do more and more of the farm work, which he disliked intensely. "Milk is a mess" and "chickens are for hawks" were two remarks he later made about farm life. As a youngster, he displayed a mechanical knack, but was only able to indulge it at night. He played with watches after his father was asleep. Ford's father heartily disapproved of his son's mechanical interests.

In 1879, when he was sixteen, Ford left home and actually walked to Detroit. Penniless and desperate for work, he landed two jobs: as an apprentice in a shop that repaired steam engines during the day, and as a repairer of watches at night. He worked eighty hours a week, receiving a mere $2.50 a week for his day job and only $2 a week for repairing watches. After a year, he moved to the Flower Brothers Machine Shop. From there he went to the Detroit Drydock Company where, at the age of seventeen, he became a machinist. As he moved from job to job, he mastered more and more of the machinist's craft.

FORD HAS HIS VISION

In 1885, Ford had the first insight that would eventually lead him to found Ford Motor Company. While repairing an internal combustion engine, he realized that by putting an internal combustion engine could power a machine for people to ride. This was not an entirely original idea. Many people had begun to experiment with "horseless carriages," both in America and Europe. But Ford's vision also included the idea of mass-producing them. He wanted to make motorized cars so cheaply that the average person could purchase one.

After several years of life in the big city, Ford returned to his father's farm. He worked cutting timber on the forty acres his father gave him and repaired farm machinery for the neighbors. In his spare time, Ford tried to build a tractor. After much effort, he built a one-cylinder steam tractor. But he was unable to develop a boiler light enough to make it practical. It was this experience that convinced him to investigate the possibilities of the gasoline engine. He began studying scientific periodicals, attempting to learn more about the internal combustion engine that he hoped to use to propel a horseless carriage. For the next several years, he tried to build his own gasoline engine.

In 1889, Ford married Clara Bryant, a neighborhood farm girl, and started to raise a family. Since marriage led to increased expenses, Ford moved his family to Detroit.

There, in 1890, he got a job with the Detroit Edison Company as an engineer and machinist. His salary was $45 a month.

FORD'S FIRST GAS BUGGY

In his spare time Ford continued to work on building a horseless carriage in his backyard. In 1892 he succeeded in developing a "gas buggy." The door of his workshed was too small for his invention to pass through, so Ford broke down the wall and pushed his invention out into the street. The first "Ford" was on the road! He put almost 1000 miles on it driving around Detroit. It was the first car in a city that was destined to become synonymous with automobiles. Ford sold it for $200 to raise funds to build a lighter version.

Meanwhile, his career was advancing at the Detroit Edison Company. By 1896, he had become the chief engineer at a salary of $125 month. To make extra money to support his research on the automobile, he taught night school. Much of this money went into financing his experiments on gasoline engines. Although Henry tried to interest his employers in helping him build a horseless carriage, they discouraged him by predicting that a gasoline engine would never be practical.

THOMAS EDISON ENCOURAGES FORD

In 1896 Ford met the great inventor Thomas Edison. In a brief conversation about Ford's work on the gasoline engine, Edison encouraged him, saying: "There is a big future for any light-weight engine that can develop a high horsepower and is self-contained ... keep on with your engine. If you can get what you are after, I can see a great future." This conversation with Edison gave Ford the courage to persevere through what were to be some very bleak years.

In 1899, Detroit Edison offered to make Ford the superintendent of the company, but only if he'd give up work on the gasoline engine. He refused. Instead, he decided to go into business for himself. He raised enough money from backers to form the Detroit Automotive Company. One of his backers was the mayor of the city. The company built twenty-five cars, but failed to survive.

Ford started again in 1901 by forming the Henry Ford Motor Company. Ford only owned one-sixth of the company, though, and soon found himself in conflict with his backers. Ford foresaw that, to be successful, the auto industry would have to produce large quantities of cars at low prices. His backers viewed the automobile as a luxury item for wealthy people.

The backers brought Henry Leland, an expert on the latest production methods, into the company. Leland had learned his craft in the firearms industry and knew a great deal about the value of the interchangeability of the parts. Unfortunately, Ford and Leland didn't get along. Ford left the company in 1902. Ironically, Leland went on to help build both Cadillac Motors and Lincoln. Cadillac was eventually sold to General Motors but Lincoln was sold to Ford.

FORD'S RACE CAR BEATS THE AMERICAN SPEED RECORD

After leaving the company, Ford rented a one-story shed and spent the entire year of 1902 working on his gasoline motors. During this time, he built two racing cars: the "999" and the "Arrow." The 999 won every race it entered and made its driver, Barney Oldfield, a national hero. Ford himself also became famous when he raced Alexander Winton, the holder of the American speed record, and beat him. At age of 40, Ford had had two major business failures. Nevertheless, he believed that, "Failure is a chance to begin again more intelligently," so in 1903 he started a third company.

The positive publicity resulting from his racing success enabled Ford to raise $28,000 from friends and neighbors. He and A.Y. Malcomson, a coal dealer, each owned 25.5 percent of the Ford Motor Company. The remaining 49 percent was divided among ten other investors. These included the Dodge brothers, whose machine shop was to supply most of the parts, and Albert Strelow, who allowed the company to use his refurbished woodworking shop as the factory. In Ford's lifetime, the firm never raised additional capital through the sale of stock.

SUCCESS AT LAST!

The company was a tremendous success from the first week. Using the strategy of simplicity, high quality and low price, Ford was able to sell 1,745 cars in 1904. From the beginning, Ford began to buy back shares from the other stockholders. By 1906 Ford owned 58.5% of the stock. Against the wishes of the other shareholders, he had the company develop the Model N, which retailed for $600. The Model N was a big success. In the year 1906-07 Ford Motor sold 9,000 cars and had revenues of $5.8 million.

In 1907, deciding that the Model N needed improvement, Ford began work on the legendary Model T. He believed there existed a tremendous demand for an inexpensive, durable automobile. But he was somewhat frustrated in his efforts by the lack of a light, strong steel. One day he picked up a piece of a French racing car that had crashed in Florida. This was a piece of vanadium steel. It was light and strong, but was not at that time being manufactured in the United States.

Ford's discovery of this material opened the modern era of mass production. The Model T was ready on October 1, 1908. By the end of 1909, 10,600 had been sold. The Model T became a worldwide success. Henry Ford became a legend in his own time—and one of the richest men of this century.

THE ASSEMBLY LINE

To keep the price of the Model T low, Ford concentrated on increasing manufacturing efficiency. Soon the Ford Motor Company had developed and perfected the assembly line. This revolutionized industry by introducing the concept of mass production. (It is said that Ford got the idea for the assembly line by watching the disassembly of hog carcasses as they came down a packing-plant trolley.)

The Ford assembly line was based on four simple principles: 1) The assigned work should be brought to the worker; 2) All work should be done waist high so that the worker doesn't have to lift; 3) Each task must be reduced to its simplest form so as to avoid human error; and 4) Human and mechanical motion should be minimized.

These principles made production fast and easy. It also bored and frustrated workers, because they were reduced to repeating the same task over and over day in and day out. Despite the obvious advantages of the assembly line, it is no coincidence that labor unrest in the '20s and '30s began in industries that employed the assembly line.

Henry Ford was outspoken and active in politics. In 1915 he was persuaded by a group of pacifists to go to Europe and help end World War I. Ford chartered an ocean liner and vowed to "get the boys out of the trenches by Christmas." The mission, of course, was a failure and Ford returned home. In 1918, Ford ran for the U.S. Senate as a Democrat from Michigan. He lost by 4,000 votes in a state that generally went Republican by 100,000 votes.

The economic crisis of 1920-21 found Ford in a precarious situation. The company had $58 million of obligations coming due between January 1st and April 18th, and there was only $20 million in cash in the bank. A major New York bank offered Ford assistance if it could take control of the company. Ford showed the banker the door without saying a word. In the next three months, Ford raised $68 million, leaving him with $30 million more than he needed. Twenty-five million was raised by selling cars to dealers, $28 million through improved production methods, and $15 million through sales of non-automotive products.

SUCCESS THROUGH PAYING GOOD WAGES AND LOWERING COST TO CONSUMER

By 1927, 15 million Fords had been sold. In the company's first twenty-four years, the worth of the original $28,000 investment had risen to $715 million. During this incredible expansion, Ford established two principles that have guided the company to this day. One was the payment of high wages to its employees to attract the "best and the brightest." The second was the lowering of costs through improved production methods.

By 1927, the cost of a Model T to the consumer had fallen from $850 to $263. In 1914, Ford was paying its workers $5 for an eight-hour day; most firms were paying only $2.40 for a nine-hour day. By 1924, Ford was manufacturing two-thirds of all cars, and in 1925 production had reached two million vehicles. The Chevrolet, General Motors' low-priced entry, began to gain on Ford, though, primarily because GM had hit on the idea of changing the appearance of its models every year to appeal to consumers. But Ford refused to change the appearance of the Model T.

Worried by Chevrolet's gains, Ford closed most of his assembly plants for all of 1927 in order to retool for the Model A. During this time, General Motors picked up many of Ford's customers. Although the Model A was successful—1.4 million were sold in 1929 — Ford began to lose money. From 1927 until 1933, Ford lost close to $85 million. By 1932 the company was forced to lower the daily wage of its workers from $5 a day to $4. The company remained in poor financial shape until 1946, when, under the guidance of Henry Ford II, the company once again became profitable. A major reason for the problems had been the lack of accounting controls. Henry Ford II realized this and brought in some of the best financial executives in the world to run the company.

Henry Ford died on April 6, 1947 on his estate at Fairlane, near Dearborn. His career is a brilliant example of the value of persistence. Had Ford given up after his first two business failures, how different the American auto industry might have been! As Henry himself often said, "Failure is just a resting place."

FOR MORE ABOUT HENRY FORD

Company Web Site: www.ford.com

Wheels Of Time: A Biography Of Henry Ford by Catherine Grouley

Bill Gates

MICROSOFT INC.: THE RICHEST MAN IN AMERICA WHO PLANS TO GIVE IT ALL AWAY

Bill Gates was born on Oct. 28, 1955, and grew up in Seattle with his parents and two sisters. Fascinated by computers, he was programming them by the time he was thirteen. Gates went to Harvard University in 1973. While a student there he developed the programming language BASIC for the first microcomputer, the MITS Altair. In 1975 he started Microsoft with his friend Paul Allen. Gates dropped out of Harvard his junior year to devote his full attention to developing user-friendly software for personal computers.

*"The bottom line is that **business** is going to **change more** in the next ten years than it has in the last fifty."*

Like the founders of Apple Computer, Inc., Stephan Wozniak and Steve Jobs, Gates believed that one day there would be a personal computer in every office and home in America. Apple planned to provide the computers; Gates was intent on supplying the software to run them.

GATES DECIDES TO BECOME THE SOFTWARE KING

Gates was also determined to find new markets by making his software so easy and fun to use that people who had never dreamed they could operate a computer would realize that they could.

Jobs and Wozniak were the hardware kings, so Gates resolved to be the software king. In those days, software — the programs that made computers do things — was not considered an important business. Software was boring. It was more often given away or traded than sold.

Gates' great insight was to commercialize software. He hired brilliant young people like himself to design software that made computers do things ordinary working people wanted them to do — calculate budgets, display them, edit manuscripts, add graphics. Gates made his software colorful and easy to use. He packaged it attractively. Gates made software fun, and consumers ate it up. By 1992, Microsoft was worth $22 billion, and Bill Gates was worth over $7 billion. At 36, he was the richest person in America.

The best entrepreneurs love risk and adventure, and possess great vision and drive. Bill Gates has these qualities in spades. He has used them, along with his formidable brainpower, to build Microsoft Corporation into one of the most powerful players in the computer industry and to make himself the richest person in America while still in his thirties. He even replaced the man he had admired as a teen, Steve Jobs, as the media's designated personal computer visionary.

A BRILLIANT PROGRAMMER AND SMART NEGOTIATOR

In 1980, when Bill Gates was only twenty-four, he conducted one of the most important negotiations of his life with one of the most powerful companies in the world, IBM. IBM was interested in having Microsoft work with it on IBM's top secret effort to develop a personal computer. No doubt, "Big Blue," as IBM was known, expected little

Microsoft, which was a $7 million company with fewer than forty employees at the time, to be a pushover. After all, IBM's annual revenues were hitting $30 billion.

Before his negotiations with IBM, however, Gates set his goals and organized his thoughts. He knew exactly what he wanted to achieve and just what his boundaries were. IBM offered to pay Microsoft $175,000 for an operating system for IBM's new personal computers called MS DOS. Gates wasn't willing to sell his company's program code for that price, however, because he knew IBM would want to use the code on a variety of future machines. Gates decided he would hold out for royalties and retain ownership of MS DOS. He also wanted to retain the right to license copies of the program's code to other parties. Later, IBM was to regret its failure to purchase MS DOS outright, as the licensing deal ended up costing Big Blue a lot of money.

During the negotiations with IBM, Gates stuck to his plan. Despite the nervousness he felt inside about negotiating with IBM, Gates gave clear, calm presentations to IBM executives regarding the operating system that Microsoft proposed to supply IBM. Gates had jeopardized deals in the past with customers and suppliers by being too intense and too eager to win.

This time, he knew he would have to make the deal worthwhile to IBM for it to succeed. IBM's representative, Sandy Meade, was surprised by Gates's boldness on the royalty issue. Meade recalled in the book *Gates* by Stephen Manes and Paul Andrews (Touchstone, 1994) that, unlike other software companies with which IBM had negotiated, "I never felt they [Microsoft] needed the money."

Meade's negotiating tactic was to remind Gates that his relationship with IBM was a "long-term relationship with the potential for big business." Gates had guessed correctly that IBM would be willing to pay royalties to use Microsoft program code in IBM's personal computers. In return for IBM's agreeing to pay royalties, Microsoft committed to a brutal delivery schedule. Gates was in the habit of having dinner at his parents' home on Sunday nights. After he signed the deal with IBM, Gates told his mother not to expect him for at least six months.

THE "MICRO-KIDS"

By the end of 1982, however, the age of the personal computer had arrived and millions of people wanted software to run their new gadgets. Revenues at Microsoft were up to $34 million and over 200 people were working for the company. Gates developed a reputation for hiring the best and the brightest and running them ragged. The press called his employees "Micro-kids." The youthful employees dressed in jeans and sneakers and conducted plastic sword fights in the hallways.

Despite the hectic pace, Gates kept his vision in mind: People want easy-to-use software. This vision led to the development of Windows, a software program whose graphics were so easy to understand that someone with no experience on a computer could figure out how to use it by trial and error.

MICROSOFT WINDOWS IS LAUNCHED

Gates rolled out Microsoft Windows on May 22, 1990, before a throng of press, analysts, and industry watchers. He was just 34, and a multibillionaire. He was also taking on IBM once again. Gates had tried to sell Windows to IBM, with whom he had a partnership, but IBM had turned him down and was developing its own competitive software, called OS/2.

Like many of Gates's pet projects, Windows was enormously risky, but the reward was great. Gates used his company's power to try to gobble up his competition and make Windows the industry standard. His competitors responded with a price war. As profits on software sales fell, Gates expanded into other computer-related developments, such as faxing and the information highway. Microsoft programmers continue to hack out new or improved programs to help consumers use the latest advances in the fast-moving digital universe. The 1995 version of Windows, for example, included software for running a modem and getting online. To get corporate America to embrace it, Microsoft gave Ford Motor Co. over 5,000 free Windows 95 licenses in return for Ford's commitment to praise the operating system to the press before its official release date. Now Microsoft is launching Windows 2000 and Gates has personally called on big customers like Chase Manhattan bank and Nissan in efforts to ensure their commitment to the new system. He kicked off a 30-city tour to teach 15,000 system builders nationwide how to install and manage Windows 2000 [*PC Week Online*, Oct. 29, "Bill Gates Faces His Greatest Challenge yet" by Joseph Panettieri and Mary Jo Foley]. He also took a moment to celebrate the fact that Microsoft was added to the Dow Jones Industrial Average in October, 1999.

In a typically non-conformist move, Gates announced that even though his stock was now going to be one of the 30 stocks that make up the legendary Dow Jones index, he had no intention of moving from the Nasdaq Stock Market to the New York Stock Exchange. "It's a milestone for the Dow Jones Industrial Average to include some technology stocks," Gates said, "It's sort of a recognition of what's already taken place in the economy." [*Bloomberg News Service*, Oct. 29, 1999, "Gates Says Microsoft Won't Move From Nasdaq To NYSE"]

Gates may be traveling on his birthday touting Windows 2000, but lately he's tempered his laser focus on Microsoft with another challenge—giving a way his huge fortune. In September, 1998, the 43-year-old Gates donated $15 billion of his estimated $72.5 billion fortune to his new charitable foundation, The Bill & Melinda Gates Foundation. Gates and his wife Melinda have stated that Gates intends to continue contributing to the foundation as part of his long-term plan to eventually give away most of his wealth [*ZDNet News*, Sept. 28, 1999, "Gates' Microsoft Stake Falls To $72.5B," by Reuters]. Gates' gift reduced his share of Microsoft from 19.8% to 15.3%, but failed to make a dent in his standing as the world's richest man.

Gates has indicated that his foundation will focus on health and education. The foundation has already committed over $300 million to global health organizations and over $300 million to educational initiatives like the Gates Library Initiative to bring computers and Internet access to low income communities in the U.S. and Canada. Gates is interested not only in technology training, but in entrepreneurship education, for young people. Microsoft is sponsoring a NFTE program in Seattle, as well as a high-tech center for young entrepreneurs in Boston. He's a big proponent of "asynchronous learning," which is online teaching that allows each student to move at his or her own pace. Gates will no doubt bring the same passion for innovation and creative solutions to his charitable work as he does to running Microsoft.

MORE ABOUT BILL GATES

Company Web Site: www.microsoft.com

The Road Ahead by Bill Gates, Penguin, 1995

Business @ the Speed of Thought by Bill Gates, Warner Books, 1999

Gates: How Microsoft's Mogul Reinvented An Industry—And Made Himself The Richest Man In America by Stephan Manes and Paul Andrews, Touchstone, 1994

King C. Gillette

GILLETTE: PERSEVERANCE ON THE CUTTING EDGE

Like many other large corporations, The Gillette Company was built around the dream of one individual. Gillette is a multi-billion dollar worldwide corporation, yet its founder once wrote that competition was the root of all evil. He felt that doing away with it would eliminate injustice, poverty and crime.

"[My invention] came more in pictures than in thought, as though the razor were already a finished thing and held before my eyes. I stood there before the mirror in a trance of joy at what I saw."

King Camp Gillette was born in Fond du Lac, Wisconsin, on January 2, 1855. When he was four, his family moved to Chicago. His father, George, worked as a patent agent and had launched two wholesale hardware businesses. He encouraged his sons to work with their hands and to learn how things worked. Efficiency and independence were key traits in the Gillette family. George was an inventor himself and held several patents.

After losing nearly all he had in the disastrous Chicago fire of 1871, George Gillette moved his family to New York. There he and the two eldest sons started a hardware supply business. Showing the independence of spirit that would mark his entire career, King stayed in Chicago, becoming a clerk in a hardware house. At twenty-one, he became a traveling salesman for a Kansas City firm.

28 YEARS AS A TRAVELING SALESMAN AND INVENTOR

For the next twenty-eight years Gillette made his living as a traveling salesman. In his spare time he invented gadgets, such as valves for water taps and conduits for electrical cables. None of these patents made him any money, however.

Gillette was a star salesman. His company thought well enough of him to send him to London to market Sapolio, a popular household scouring powder. In 1890, Gillette returned to the States and got married. The following year he joined the Baltimore Seal Company as the sales representative for New York and New England.

The president of the company, William Painter, was an inventor who had developed a bottle-stopper consisting of a cork-lined tin cap. Unlike Gillette, Painter's inventions had made him money. Once he offhandedly suggested to Gillette that he try to think of something that was used once and then thrown away. That way the customer would have to keep coming back for more. Painter's words stayed with Gillette and soon became an obsession with him. He would go through the alphabet each day, hoping that the letters would inspire him to invent a way to improve something that people used frequently.

GILLETTE'S MOMENT OF INSPIRATION

While he was shaving one morning in 1895, Gillette was finally struck by the inspiration for which he'd been praying. Like a sculptor who stares at a block of marble and sees an unborn statue, he gazed at his old, dull razor and wondered: Would it be possible to make razor blades so cheaply that the user could replace dull blades with new ones and thereby do away with the task of sharpening them? In a flash, he had the insight that a wafer-thin razor blade would be the answer. Gillette later described this insight: "In that moment...I could see the way the blade could be held in a holder, then came the idea of sharpening the two opposite edges on the thin piece of steel...thus doubling its service. All this came more in pictures than in thought, as though the razor were already a finished thing and held before my eyes. I stood there before the mirror in a trance of joy at what I saw."

THE REVOLUTIONARY GILLETTE SAFETY RAZOR HAD BEEN CONCEIVED.

Before the safety razor, shaving had been a hazardous and unpleasant experience for men. In prehistoric times, men scraped away their beards with clamshells, sharpened animal teeth, or flint. For centuries, few men would submit themselves to a barber every single day. In the Middle Ages, a well-groomed man shaved twice a week. In Elizabethan England, a beard was considered more than two weeks' growth. Even by the 19th century, no razor had been produced that was much better than medieval models, in spite of the improvement of using steel.

YEARS OF STRUGGLE DEVELOPING MODELS AND MACHINERY

Gillette constructed a crude model that failed miserably when tested. But he remained determined. Frustrating years of struggle lay ahead. Experts insisted that a sharp edge could not be put on sheet steel.

In 1899 Gillette brought his drawings to Steven Porter, a Boston machinist. Porter turned out three razors and several blades. But obstacles remained to be overcome. The machinery needed to mass-produce the models did not yet exist.

Then Gillette met William Nickerson, a more accomplished innovator and inventor than he was. After studying the razor, Nickerson said he could design and build the necessary machinery for about $5,000. As compensation, he would accept stock in the yet-to-be-formed corporation. He agreed to devote half his working day to developing the equipment necessary to turning out the blades and razors.

By 1901, Gillette and Nickerson had gained the interest of financiers Jacob Heilborn and Edward Stewart. They capitalized the new company at $500,000 and divided it into 50,000 shares at $10 each. Gillette received 17,500 shares and 12,500 were split among the other three partners. Twenty thousand shares remained in the company's treasury.

In 1901, as the machinery neared completion, Gillette changed the name of the company from the American Safety Razor Company to the Gillette Safety Razor Company.

Eventually, the company logo included Gillette's picture. This exposure made the inventor (in those pre-TV days) one of the best-known faces in America.

The future seemed bright, but before long the company was $12,500 in debt. When they ran low on capital, the founders started selling 500-share blocks for $250. (In one case, this $250 investment was resold for $62,500.)

It was a difficult time. Gillette said later: "We were backed up to the wall with our creditors lined up in front waiting for the signal to fire." He wasn't ready to let his dream die, though. In 1902 he went to John Joyce, a Boston millionaire, for help. Joyce proposed that the company issue $100,000 worth of eight-percent bonds which he would then buy at 60 cents on the dollar. With Joyce's money, Nickerson was able to finish the sharpening machine and begin turning out sample razors and blades.

PUBLIC RESPONSE TO THE SAFETY RAZOR WAS POOR AT FIRST

The public got a look at the razor in a half-page ad in *System* magazine. The ad asked for $5 for the product, and read, "You'll have to see it to appreciate it." Public response was almost zero. By 1903, only 51 razors had been sold by mail. By June of 1904, Joyce was disturbed by the small output of the factory in which he had invested $60,000. Faulty machines were ruining a great number of blades. It was a difficult task to produce the 1,250 sets needed to break even each week.

But later that year, the U.S. Patent Office granted Gillette exclusive rights to his "new and useful improvements in razors." Working under pressure now, Nickerson developed a new blade-grinding process that rescued the company. With the factory straightened out, sales began to soar. By the end of 1904, Gillette's annual production had grown to 250,000 razor sets and an additional 100,000 blade packages. The directors bought a six-story building in South Boston the following year.

The new company excelled in distribution and advertising, the two keys to rapid sales growth. In 1904 the mail-order business ceased and Gillette razors were sold in hardware, cutlery, jewelry and sporting goods stores. Gillette paid its first cash dividend on its stock in 1906.

The next ten years saw phenomenal growth. Soon the razor sets were selling at a rate of about 350,000 a year. Sales of blade packages alone were over 7 million.

THE ARMY CLINCHES IT

In 1917 Gillette enjoyed an unforeseen major boost to its sales. The United States had entered World War I. The government was worried about unsanitary conditions in the trenches. So the Defense Department ordered 3. 5 million razors and 36 million blades. Gillette supplied nearly the entire American Expeditionary Force.

The Army's decision changed the shaving habits of millions of young Americans. When they returned home, they maintained their loyalty to the Gillette Safety Razor they had used overseas.

Sales continued to increase in the 1920s, both at home and abroad. Gillette developed popular promotions with other well-known firms. One million sets alone were distributed by the Wrigley Company when their dealers received a free razor set with the purchase of a box of Wrigley's gum.

GILLETTE 2000

King C. Gillette died on July 9, 1932 at age 77. His disposable razor is taken for granted today. But for men at the turn of the century, it was a long-awaited and welcome innovation.

Today The Gillette Company employs over 40,000 people worldwide. Sales for 1998 reached $10.1 billion. When King C. Gillette opened an office in London he probably never imagined that the company, which will celebrate its 100th anniversary in 2001, would eventually distribute its products in over 200 countries. Gillette is the world leader in male grooming products and holds the number one position in many female grooming products,
such as razors and shaving cream, as well.

Over the years, The Company has used acquisitions to become the world's top seller of writing instruments, toothbrushes, and oral care appliances. Oral B, Paper Mate, and Duracell are just some of Gillette's acquisitions.

The Gillette Company has become increasingly philanthropic in the 1990s, especially in the area of women's health. After pledging $5 million in 1977 to open the Gillette Centers for Women's Cancers, Gillette has taken its commitment to the Internet in 1999 by developing the Gillette Women's Cancer Connection (www.gillettecancerconnect.org) to provide women battling cancer with support and resources.

MORE ABOUT KING C. GILLETTE

Company Web Site: www.gillette.com

King C. Gillette, The Man and His Wonderful Shaving Device by Russell B. Adams (out of print)

Berry Gordy

MOTOWN: BRINGING DETROIT SOUL TO THE WORLD

The list of artists nurtured by Berry Gordy, Jr., at Motown Records reads like the R&B Hall of Fame: The Supremes, the Miracles, Marvin Gaye, Stevie Wonder, the Jackson 5, the Temptations, the Four Tops, the Miracles. Today Motown is home to hitmakers like Boyz II Men, Queen Latifah, and Brian McKnight. Gordy brought soul to America—to both black and white America. And under his direction Motown became a model of black capitalism, as well one of the most important forces on the American music scene.

"There aren't enough people who care about the future. They are too busy worrying about today and what they can grab now."

Nothing in Gordy's upbringing prepared him for such stunning success. He was born in 1929 in a Detroit ghetto. One of eight children, he had to make do with hand-me-downs and learn to survive in a tough neighborhood. During his teenage years, Gordy developed a deep desire to escape from the misery and poverty that surrounded him. He was unsure which path would serve this purpose. He was a strong athlete who also enjoyed pop music and songwriting. The fields of sports or music seemed to him, therefore, to be the most logical avenues to pursue.

THE YOUNG BOXER

Because he grew up in a rough neighborhood, Gordy often had to defend himself by fighting. He decided to make boxing his profession. He began training in neighborhood gyms, until he found a manager who got him into professional fights. Although Gordy won ten out of fourteen fights as a featherweight, he became disillusioned with the life of a boxer. He was also dissatisfied with the lack of financial reward in the featherweight class. Nevertheless, the life of a boxer taught him discipline and drive—lessons that benefited him throughout his entire career.

Gordy's next venture was to open a jazz record shop. It soon went bankrupt. But he refused to let himself become discouraged. He turned to various day jobs; at the same time, he was also writing songs for local acts.

Finally Gordy decided to take a job on the assembly line at Ford Motor Company, as a chrome trimmer. Although he made only $85 a week, the job taught him the value of strict quality control—something that proved vital to his record-making career. During his spare time, he worked on songs and went to nightclubs. He listened to performers and discussed the music industry with anyone he could find in the field.

OFF TO NEW YORK TO SELL SONGS

Music was Gordy's true passion. In fact, he had been writing songs since his early twenties. He saved some money from his job and took off for New York to try make contacts with people in the recording industry and music publishing. After a series of rejections, he finally started to sell a few songs in the mid-1950s. A few became hits in the R&B (Rhythm and Blues) category.

Gordy's first national success came when he was 28 and Jackie Wilson made his song

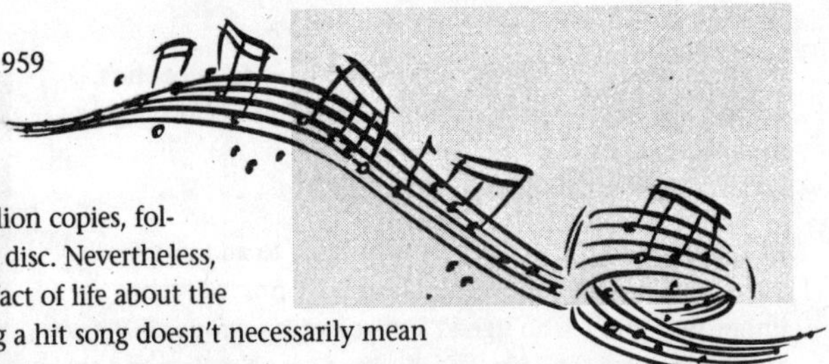

"Reet Petite" a hit. In 1959 another Gordy tune, "Lonely Teardrops, " sold a million copies, followed by another gold disc. Nevertheless, Gordy learned a hard fact of life about the music business: writing a hit song doesn't necessarily mean tapping into a gold mine.

By the late 1950s, Gordy was back in Detroit, working on the assembly line at Ford. As he described his situation to one reporter: "I was broke even with the hit records in certain cases. By the time the records would be hits, I would get the money but my end of it would be so small that I'd always be broke," he recalls. "When the companies finally paid me, it was three months later and I owed money out to the family."

GORDY BECOMES AN ENTREPRENEUR

Maybe, Gordy realized, he could make a living in the record business if he produced records himself and kept control of the music.

To pursue his dream, Gordy borrowed $700 from his sister, Anna. He invested this $700 in setting up a makeshift recording studio in a run-down section of Detroit. Luckily for him; Detroit was filled with gifted black musicians eager for a break. Many were from the ghetto themselves. He began to hold talent hunt auditions for his new company, which he called Motown Records (for Detroit, the Motor Town — the capital of car manufacturing). Gordy's task was to match singers with songwriters, producers, managers and other musicians he himself knew. From the beginning, he had a talent for finding and then blending talents.

He also had plenty of nerve and persistence. While others called Motown Records an upstart company, Gordy conceived of it as the channel for "the Sound of Young America." If, to some, Motown's first headquarters was an old run-down house, to Gordy it was mission control of "Hitsville U.S.A." He slept on the floor above his recording studio.

THE MOTOWN FAMILY

When he set up his own company in late '58, he organized it as a "family." His songwriters and producers lived and worked together at the same location. Gordy made every decision based on the long-term consequences: "There aren't enough people who care about the future," he said. "They are too busy worrying about today and what they can grab now. If I deal with a person, I have to know he's going to be happy ten years from now." This philosophy was destined to carry him straight to the top.

In 1959, one of the performers who came to audition was a 19-year-old named Smokey Robinson. He immediately impressed Gordy, who signed Smokey with a group of Detroit teenagers called the Miracles. Within a year, Smokey and the Miracles yielded two major hits.

He used the profits to add to his list of performing artists. During 1961-62, he signed contracts with such promising newcomers as the Supremes, Martha and the Vandellas, the Temptations, and Marvin Gaye. Soon, Motown attracted Stevie Wonder, the Four Tops, Junior Walker and the All Stars, and many other great artists. Gordy also hired a team of top-flight producers and songwriters.

In 1966, Gordy had fourteen records reach the Top 10 list. Many of Motown's recordings are still classics today, among them the hits by the Four Tops ("Reach Out, I'll Be There"), the Temptations ("My Girl"), and the Supremes ("Stop! In the Name of Love").

THE MOTOWN SOUND

Gordy realized that America's youth wanted to dance—and he gave them the driving beat they wanted."The Motown Sound" was instantly recognizable in the world of American pop music. A wide variety of factors made it irresistible to young people: a driving beat, strong emotions, polish, its combination of sweetness and soulfulness, and powerful bass lines.

Motown's appeal was universal; both blacks and whites immediately responded to it. Gordy once estimated that for one of the Miracles' hits, "Shop Around," African-Americans bought only half the number of recordings as white teenagers.

Like the Detroit assembly line where he had once worked, Gordy ground out a stream of first-class products—now-classic recordings that became known as "The Sound of Young America." He had an astonishing 110 No. 1 hits.

His recording successes led to other ventures — the packaging of his acts into slick road shows known as the Motown Revue and TV specials featuring Motown artists.

Throughout the '60s, Gordy enjoyed huge financial — and creative — successes. But these successes were built on constantly refining his entrepreneurial standards and abilities. He kept a close watch on all the music produced by his company. He truly molded the unique Motown Sound. Such tight creative control was based on powerful practical reasons. As Gordy expressed it, "We were undercapitalized. All our records had to be hits, because we couldn't afford any flops."

In an interview, Gordy commented on one of his major principles as an entrepreneur in the recording business: "We've developed and discovered every artist we've had. We never bought an artist who was already at the top. We took the kids off the street. If they're good enough, we advance them the money and work with them."

QUALITY OVER QUANTITY

Foremost among his business principles was an insistence on quality over quantity. Gordy devoted himself to the development of his artists' gifts. He pushed his artists to improve their skills and polish their talents constantly. At recording sessions, both he and his associates demanded the highest of standards in both performance and recording techniques. Gordy listened to every track his engineers made. Cuts had to be rerecorded time and time again until he was completely satisfied.

Because ot his constant striving for perfection, the number of singles issued by Motown in the '60s was among the lowest in the recording industry The percentage of these singles which went on to become hits, though, was one of the highest.

During the '60s, Motown's rise to fame was earned through over 120 Top Twenty hits. The company dominated the Soul market. By the early '70s, Motown and its associated ventures were one of the top ten enterprises in the recording field. Company sales exceeded $10 million a year.

Added to its roster of artists were such superstars as Michael Jackson and Lionel Ritchie. Motown even expanded into movies and live theater. It was the driving force behind the hit movie, "Lady Sings the Blues," starring Diana Ross as the legendary Billie Holiday. Ross was Motown's biggest superstar. Motown moved to California in the early '70s in part to get Ross into the movies.

Although the distinctive Motown Sound eventually faded, the label continued to prosper through sales from such artists as Stevie Wonder and Marvin Gaye, both of whom gained artistic control over their recordings. By 1977, Tamla-Motown (Tamla being a sister label) was the largest African-American-owned conglomerate in America.

LOSING ARTISTS TO BIGGER LABELS

However, in the late '70s and early '80s, many of Motown's superstars, like Diana Ross, Gladys Knight and the Pips, Michael Jackson, and Marvin Gaye left for other labels. There were signs that Motown was losing some of its former glory. Gordy denied this, saying, "I'm as excited today as I was in the beginning. We've got new roads...the cable, the technology of the computer, digital recordings. We've got more movies to make, too."

In many ways, his optimism was well founded. In 1983, Motown revenues were $104 million. Gordy lived in a hilltop estate and Motown's offices occupied three floors of a high-rise in Hollywood. Two hundred employees staffed an entertainment empire that included TV and movie production, as well as music publishing.

Gordy's optimism was admirable but not realistic. In mid-1988, the company was sold to MCA Records and the investment company, Boston Ventures, for $61 million. A landmark era in American popular music had ended.

By the late 1990s, however, Motown had got its groove back under the leadership of Andre Harrell, who was only 35 when he was appointed to rebuild the company—with Gordy's blessing. Harrell, a hip hop producer and former president of Uptown records, who launched big sellers there like Mary J. Blige and Jodeci, was determined to renew R&B by injecting it with hip hop flavor. Gordy's genius had brought R&B, Soul, and gospel into the American pop-music mainstream. In the process, he made a noble contribution to the "desegregation" of American pop music. Gordy told him: "Don't second guess yourself. Just follow your instincts," [*Detroit News*, "Will Motown Get Its Groove Back?" by Ruby Bailey, May 16, 1996]. Harrell scored hits with Boyz II Men and an updated Motown R&B sound was born. The label has been renewed with TV specials that both pay tribute to its past and hype its future.

MORE ABOUT BERRY GORDY

Company Web Site: www.motown.com

The Songs of Berry Gordy; The Music, The Magic, The Memories of Motown by Jeanette Delissa, July 1995

John Johnson

JOHNSON PUBLISHING COMPANY: VISIONARY BEHIND EBONY AND JET

The man who would become the owner of the world's largest Black-owned publishing company was born into segregation on June 19, 1918 in Arkansas City, Arkansas. His father, a mill worker, died when he was six. The boy was raised by his mother and stepfather.

Arkansas City's only high school was open to "whites only." For this reason, John and his mother moved north to Chicago for his secondary school education. In high school, he not only edited both the school's newspaper and yearbook but also was an honors graduate. In addition, he served as president of both the student council and the senior class.

*"Once you achieve a small **dream** and make a small **success**, it gives you **confidence** to go on to the next step."*

After high-school graduation, an insurance executive happened to hear a speech delivered by Johnson. He was so impressed he offered Johnson a partial scholarship at the University of Chicago. After two years, Johnson left the University. He transferred to the Northwestern School of Commerce, where he studied for two more years before joining the Supreme Liberty Life Insurance Company.

JOHNSON'S FIRST MAGAZINE FOR AFRICAN-AMERICANS

Johnson wrote the Supreme Liberty Life Insurance Newsletter, but he really wanted to start a magazine for and about African Americans. He believed that a digest of weekly or monthly news stories of particular interest to the African-American community could attract a lot of readers.

To finance his enterprise, Johnson first approached friends and businessmen in Chicago. They all turned down his requests for a loan. Help finally came from his mother, a seamstress. She pawned her household furniture to raise $500. In 1942, Johnson and his mother entered the publishing business.

Their publication, *Negro Digest,* contained news reprints as well as feature articles of particular interest and importance to African Americans. Among the feature articles, the one that most stimulated circulation was entitled "If I Were a Negro," by Eleanor Roosevelt.

Before the first issue appeared, Johnson mailed 20,000 letters in an attempt to obtain charter memberships at the rate of $2 each. This effort resulted in 3,000 subscribers. Johnson actually gave money to friends to buy copies of the magazine so he could convince distributors to carry it. After just one year, the magazine was selling at a rate of 50,000 copies a month.

EBONY

In 1945 Johnson decided to test the market with another publication called *Ebony*. It was a glossy-paper picture magazine patterned after the famous *Life*. The very first issue sold out its initial press run of 25,000 copies.

As large companies began to advertise regularly, *Ebony* became a staple on the news-stands and in the world of journalism. To promote his magazine, Johnson ran ads both for consumer merchandise and ethnic products. These products were mostly hair- and skin-conditioning products for African-Americans.

EBONY®

At first Ebony focused on glamour and flashy photographs, but it developed into a family-oriented publication. It showcased African-American success stories and profiled African-American entertainers. In every way—style, tone and format—*Ebony* stressed "the good life" that could be available to African Americans. This was very appealing to middle-class citizens who were already reaping the rewards of "The American Dream." But it also offered valuable role models to poor people who aspired to economic security. For a while, the magazine alienated many African-American activists, who felt *Ebony* was superficial. Gradually, though, the magazine became more socially conscious.

USING MAGAZINES TO PROMOTE OTHER BUSINESSES

In 1990, its circulation exceeded 1.5 million. Johnson's empire has expanded to include two other magazines, *Jet*, and *Ebony Man*, as well as book publishing. Johnson has wisely used his three magazines to promote his other businesses, including Supreme Life Insurance Co., the *Ebony/Jet* Showcase (a nationally syndicated television program) and Supreme Beauty Products. Johnson hopes to initiate a series of books on black celebrities in entertainment, sports and politics.

His empire also includes a nationally syndicated television program and two radio stations. One of them, WJPC-AM, was Chicago's first and only African-American-owned radio station. It is a major source of both music and information for Chicago's African-American community. Johnson also owns Fashion Fair Cosmetic Company, which is run by his wife, Eunice, and several skyscraper office buildings. The Fashion Fair cosmetics line is carried by over 1,500 stores worldwide. In addition, Johnson is principal stockholder, chairman, and chief executive officer of the Supreme Life Insurance Company.

DREAM SMALL

Johnson's headquarters are in an 11-story building in downtown Chicago. Johnson built the structure in 1972 for $7 million. It contains a permanent collection of African-American and African paintings, valued at over half a million dollars. He also maintains offices in Los Angeles, New York and Washington, D.C.

Johnson remains chairman and chief executive officer of JPC and he's constantly exploring new ventures. He doesn't believe in sitting back and enjoying his success. Instead, his motto has always been to "run scared" every business day and to use "every legal means to survive and grow." In November 1995, for example, Johnson launched *Ebony South Africa*.

About his philosophy, he said: "I always advise young people to dream small things, because small things can be achieved, and once you achieve a small dream and make a small success, it gives you confidence to go on to the next step.

"Today's entrepreneurs think too big," he added. "They want to accomplish too much. They want to put together joint ventures, conglomerates and coalitions, when in fact entrepreneurship is personal. It is what you can do almost by yourself. You can't wait around for somebody else to go in with you, because it's difficult to get a group of people to agree on one objective. And trying to get a group consensus often delays the development of really good ideas. I think we entrepreneurs have to start from where we are, with what we already have."

CREATIVE FINANCING

About trying to finance a business, he said, "I favor blacks trying to negotiate a joint venture or get loans from banks. But when all else fails, then we have to come up with creative financing, and creative financing to me means clean, legitimate ways you can get the money.

"I have never let the inability to get capital keep me from growing and surviving. I thought of all kinds of unique ways to survive. In the early days, when I could not get financing from a bank, I sold lifetime subscriptions for $100 each. Now that, in effect, is like selling stock, except you don't go through the Securities and Exchange Commission.

"Publishing depends on advertising. But Johnson has tried to avoid a dependency on outside companies in order to ensure his own success. His solution was to start his own companies to advertise in his magazines: "White advertisers would not advertise with *Ebony* in the beginning, and *Ebony*'s very survival depended on advertising, so I started a group of mail-order companies and advertised in my own magazine. The company was called Beauty Star. I sold vitamins, wigs, dresses and hair-care products. I sold anything I could sell in order to get enough capital to keep Ebony going. And I used the first $50,000 I made as a down payment on my first major building."

Johnson strongly believes that "the best and the brightest among us [should] go back to their communities and start small businesses. We have turned our backs on these so-called small businesses without realizing that these businesses can become large businesses."

PEOPLE SHOULD NOT MAKE SACRIFICES TO WORK HERE

When asked about his working relationship with his company's employees, Johnson said: "I genuinely care about the welfare of the employees. I get to know them well. I have a policy here that no one is ever employed unless I personally meet them. I learn the names of the people I come in daily contact with; I know most of their birthdays and I inquire about their families. Above all, I pay them a good salary and I give them good benefits. People should not make a sacrifice to work for a black company. A good black company has to pay good wages and offer good fringe benefits. We have to care about the people. I've had a good record of keeping good people over a long period of time."

Today Johnson regularly makes *Forbes* magazine's list of the 400 richest people in America, with an estimated net worth of approximately $100 million. But he's also rich in the esteem with which he has been held by presidents. In 1961, President John Kennedy appointed him as a Special United States Ambassador to the Ivory Coast. In 1963, President Lyndon Johnson made him Special United States Ambassador to Kenya.

Johnson has also received many honors and awards for his philanthropic, civic, cultural and business activities. He holds honorary degrees from 18 colleges and universities. Both Illinois Governor James Thompson and Chicago's Mayor Harold Washington made proclamations that declared a "John H. Johnson Day" in the City of Chicago and the State of Illinois.

In 1983, he was presented with the Chicagoan of the Year award by the Chicago Boys Club. He was the first African-American to receive this honor in the club's 82-year history. He has served as a Trustee for the Art Institute of Chicago and the United Negro College Fund. In addition, he has been on the Advisory Council of the Harvard Graduate School of Business. He serves on the boards of directors of several large corporations, including Greyhound, Verex Corporation, Marine Midland Bank, Zenith Radio Corporation and the Twentieth-Century Fox.

Through The Johnson Publishing Company, Johnson has touched the lives of millions of African Americans. He has continued to show his concern for his community by channeling his money not only into the growth of his enterprises but also into many charities that help his community, including the United Negro College Fund. Johnson is a role model for an entire generation of African-American entrepreneurs.

MORE ABOUT JOHN JOHNSON

Company Web Site: www.ebony.com, www.jetmag.com

Succeeding Against The Odds by John H. Johnson, Amisted Press, New York, 1993

Robert L. Johnson

BET HOLDINGS, INC.: AFRICAN-AMERICAN TELEVISION

When it comes to racism, Robert L. Johnson has certainly put his money where his mouth is. As president and CEO of Black Entertainment Television, Johnson has become a powerful media force, capable of directly influencing how African Americans are both perceived and portrayed by television culture. BET began its 20th season in 1999 by making the largest order for African-American movies in Hollywood history through its subsidiary, BET Arabesque Films, which will produce 10 made-for-TV movies. Johnson also added a new late night talk show, BET Live From LA, and seven other new original shows.

"Black people will become powerful in this country through control of economic wealth. You become powerful if you gain something that somebody else wants and you control it. And I believe if we did that we would be far less subject to racism."

BET is attacking racism in the media from another angle, as well. Tavis Smiley, a BET talk show host, was instrumental in coordinating 10 weeks of protests by African Americans demanding that the company advertise in black media outlets. BET is also speaking out publicly about the disparity in advertising rates between black-oriented media and similar-sized non-cable networks. Overcoming the notion that the black audience is not worth big advertising bucks will take time, but for starters Smiley appeared on radio shows urging African Americans to mail CompUSA receipts to the store, which prompted CompUSA to offer 10% discounts to those who mailed receipts [*Cable World*, "BET Seeks Fair Ad Rates" by Linda Hardesty, Nov. 1, 1999].

HEADY GROWTH

Meanwhile, BET just keeps growing. The company has morphed from a weekly, two-hour cable channel in only 3.8 million homes to a multimedia entertainment conglomerate serving over 58 million households. BET is the first, and so far the only, African-American television station that has sold shares on the New York Stock Exchange. In 1991, the year it went public (sold shares), BET earned nearly $61.7 million and reached nearly 30 million subscribers. The number of subscribers to the cable channel has since climbed to almost 40 million. All this from a company that Johnson founded in 1979 with a $15,000 loan.

Today BET Holdings, the parent company for Black Entertainment Television, publishes a magazine for African-American teenagers called YSB, owns a controlling interest in *Emerge*, a magazine for African-American professionals, and, in 1996, launched an all-jazz television channel called The Cable Jazz Channel. This outstanding performance has prompted both *Forbes* and *Business Week* to call BET one of the best small companies in America. For his efforts, Johnson has won the NAACP Image Award and the Turner Broadcasting Trumpet Award.

HARDWORKING PARENTS

The ninth of ten children, Johnson was born April 8, 1946 in a rural area called Hickory, Missouri. There was little work in Hickory, so soon the family moved to Freeport, Illinois, where both his parents found work in local factories. Johnson's hardworking parents taught him, he has said, that "nobody is going to hand deliver anything to you. You have got to do what you can do for yourself, and have a lot of confidence that you can do it."

JOHNSON WANTED TO BE A PILOT

Johnson's first goal was to become a fighter pilot for the U.S. Air Force, until he learned that twenty-twenty vision was required. Instead, he worked hard at his schoolwork. He graduated with honors from high school and won an academic scholarship to the University of Illinois, where he earned a B.A. degree in history.

After college, Johnson studied at the prestigious Woodrow Wilson School of Public and International Affairs as part of a Ford Foundation-sponsored program to attract minority students to careers in international relations. When Johnson graduated in 1972 with a master's degree in public affairs, he ranked sixth in his class.

After school Johnson moved to Washington, D.C., where he hoped to find a job, although he wasn't sure exactly what kind of career he wanted to pursue. Through a series of contacts, he landed a job as public affairs officer for the Corporation for Public Broadcasting. When he left this job, he worked as a press secretary for several politicians before being named vice-president for government relations at the National Cable Television Association (NCTA). This association represented hundreds of cable television companies to congressional representatives and senators.

While working as a lobbyist for the cable industry, Johnson learned a lot about the fledgling industry. One thing he realized was that there were many sizable markets, such as the elderly, women, and minorities, that were not being targeted by cable television channels. This was the seed of Johnson's dream for a cable station that would offer what he called "black entertainment, programming that addresses itself, in fact or in fiction, to black cultural themes and lifestyles."

RAISING CAPITAL

Johnson had no capital to launch such a costly business, however. He had such strong belief in his dream, however, that he secured a $15,000 loan from a D.C. bank, using a consulting contract he had landed as collateral.

Next, Johnson searched for an investor. He was turned down by everyone he approached until he found John C. Malone, the president of TeleCommunications, the nation's largest builder and operator of cable television systems. Malone agreed to pay $180,000 for 20 percent of Johnson's network, and loaned Johnson an additional $320,000.

The half million dollars Johnson raised was sufficient for him to start limited broadcasts using another cable channel. Starting on January 25, 1980, BET broadcast for two hours every Friday night at 11 p.m. The first movie broadcast on BET was A Visit to the Chief's Son, a movie set in Kenya. Slowly, BET added other programs to the weekly two-hour movie—African-American college football and basketball games and Video Soul, a music program featuring African-American artists. In 1982, BET began broadcasting music videos that it received free from record labels. By this time the channel was broadcasting six hours daily.

PARTNERSHIP WITH HBO

Most telecommunications ventures lose money at first, and BET was no exception. BET lost money for its first six years. To pay the bills and expand the business, Johnson found new investors. Taft Broadcasting Company became an equity partner in 1982 and HBO became a partner in 1984. In exchange for $10 million in investment, TCI, Taft, and HBO acquired a 48 percent share of BET. The HBO partnership supplied BET with a satellite it used to become a full-fledged, 24-hour network.

By 1988, BET was able to begin paying back its investors. By mid-1989, the channel was reaching 23 million homes in 1300 markets. It still was carried by very few cable systems, however. The industry was unconvinced that there was big market for BET. Johnson's business was also hampered by the low subscription fee that had been set by the NCTA. The NCTA had set BET's per subscriber fee at 2.5 cents, an amount far lower than that charged by other cable networks. This made it impossible for Johnson to afford to produce quality original shows that could draw more viewers.

Frustrated, Johnson lobbied NCTA for an increase in fees to five cents per subscriber. The increase was granted in 1989. BET opened a $10 million production facility in D.C. and began producing original shows. By 1991, BET had created 14 new shows and was attracting critical acclaim and new subscribers.

Johnson didn't stop there, however. He has often been quoted saying, "When I see BET, I don't see a cable network. I see a black media conglomerate." In 1991, he started a magazine for African-American teenagers called YSB (Young Sisters and Brothers). Within two years YSB's circulation grew to 80,000. BET also acquired a controlling interest in *Emerge* in 1991.

GOING PUBLIC

Also in 1991, Johnson decided to sell BET stock to raise capital for his new projects. On October 30, 1991 BET Holdings became the first African-American-controlled firm to be listed on the New York Stock Exchange. Trading opened at $17 per share and the price rose by the end of the day to over $23 a share. By selling 375,000 of his shares in the company, Johnson made $6.4 million that day, as the company's market value rose to $475 million.

Although investors were initially enthusiastic about BET stock, the stock had a rough ride for the first year or so. After Johnson reported disappointing earnings one quarter, the stock dropped as low as $12 per share. Johnson had to ask the NYSE to temporarily halt trading in it. Investors eventually regained confidence in the company, however, when it began posting regularly increasing revenues and profits. Today BET is the seventeenth largest African-American-owned company in the United States.

DIVERSIFYING INTO AN ENTERTAINMENT EMPIRE

The company has steadily prospered under Johnson's close guidance. He typically works fifteen hours a day, six days a week. Johnson is definitely not interested in slowing down, although he enjoys his wealth (Johnson drives a Jaguar and he and his wife and children live in a beautiful house complete with pool and tennis court in a suburb of D.C.). His real passion is diversifying his company into an entertainment empire. To that end, he launched the BET radio network in 1994, a pay-per view jazz channel, and has began limited programming in the United Kingdom, South Africa, and other parts of the world.

BET has also increased its profile greatly in the music industry. Acknowledging the impact HIV/AIDS has had on the African-American community, BET teamed with VH1, MTV, LIFEbeat, and Ticketmaster to broadcast a series of high-profile programs to educate viewers about the threat of HIV/AIDS, and net donations for LIFEbeat. In recognition of Johnson's influence in the music industry, the Rock and Roll Hall of Fame added him to its Board of Governors in 1999.

Johnson's also a jazz fan, so in 1996 he launched a new 24-hour sister cable channel devoted exclusively to jazz called BET on Jazz: The Cable Jazz Channel. The channel programs all kinds of jazz entertainment, from festival performances and music videos to documentaries. Unlike BET, BET on Jazz is not targeted to only the African-American audience. The station's programmers plan to feature "the best artists in jazz—regardless of their ethnic background."

BET is branching into music retail as well, with a direct-mail line of CDs from its long-running show "Video Soul" that it is offering in partnership with Rhino Records. Through innovative partnerships and Johnson's tireless energy and unflagging ambition, BET Holdings, Inc. should be an increasingly important player in the entertainment industry.

Company Web Site: www.betnetworks.com

Ray Kroc

MCDONALD'S

Success With Someone Else's Idea

You might think you have to come up with a completely original business idea to become an entrepreneur. But many fortunes have been built by entrepreneurs who have developed or improved upon someone else's idea. Ray Kroc made $1 billion by developing an obscure California hamburger restaurant into the McDonald's franchise empire.

*"Nothing in the world can take the place of **persistence**. Nothing is more common than unsuccessful men with talent. The world is full of educated derelicts. Persistence and determination alone are omnipotent."*

A self-made success, Kroc served briefly as an ambulance driver in France in World War I. (One of his roommates at boot camp was another successful entrepreneur, Walt Disney.) Once he returned to Illinois, much of Kroc's time was spent on the road as a traveling salesman. These experiences—combined with the meals he had consumed on the run—may have sparked his genius for the fast-food industry.

Ray's father was a real-estate broker whose family had emigrated from what is now Czechoslovakia. Ray himself, in his twenties, tried to sell real-estate in Florida, among a variety of other jobs, including playing the piano with a traveling band. But the real-estate venture was his low point. Describing his return to Chicago after going bankrupt, Kroc wrote in his autobiography, *Grinding It Out*: "I was broke. I didn't have an overcoat, a topcoat, or a pair of gloves. I drove into Chicago on icy streets. When I got home I was frozen stiff, disillusioned and depressed."

After several more years of frustrating jobs, Ray landed a position as a salesman for the Lily Tulip Cup Co. He worked for Lily as a salesman for 17 years. In 1941, he decided to open his own firm, as a distributor of Multimixers. These were so named because they mixed five malted-milk shakes at a time. For the next thirteen years he made a comfortable but unspectacular living.

A CHANCE ENCOUNTER

As is so often the case, the struggling entrepreneur has a chance encounter and sees an opportunity that becomes the basis for his fortune. For Kroc, that day came in 1954 when the 52-year-old was going over his sales reports. He noticed that the largest purchaser of his Multimixers was a restaurant in San Bernardino, run by two brothers, Mac and Dick McDonald.

Kroc decided to go to California to see the restaurant for himself. As he was later to describe it, "I had to see what kind of operation was making forty malts at a time." The first thing he noticed was that "They had people standing in line clamoring for those 15-cent hamburgers." At first Kroc encouraged the McDonald brothers to expand, thinking that if they started more restaurants, he could become wealthy supplying them with Multimixers. Dick McDonald replied by pointing to a house a short distance away: "See that house up there? That's home to me, and I like it here. If we opened a chain, I'd never be home."

Suddenly, Kroc had his entrepreneurial insight of going it alone and opening "McDonald's" all over the country. As he himself describes it: "I can't pretend to know what it is—certainly it's not some divine vision. Perhaps it's a combination of your background and experience, your instincts, and your dreams. Whatever it was, I saw it in the McDonald operation and in that moment I suppose I became an entrepreneur. I decided to go for broke." After much negotiation, Kroc bought the franchise rights to the future McDonald's chain in exchange for 1/3 of 1% of the gross receipts.

The first of Kroc's McDonald's opened in Des Plaines, a Chicago suburb, in 1955. It was an immediate success and McDonald's became one of the fastest growing businesses in America. By 1960 there were 228 McDonald's restaurants. A hundred additional McDonald's opened each year. From 1968 on, over 200 more McDonald franchises opened per year. In 1961, Ray bought out the McDonald brothers by going heavily into debt.

"PRESS ON."

During the early start-up years, when Kroc was working about 80 hours a week, his simple motto kept him going: "Press on." He has noted, "Nothing in the world can take the place of persistence. Talent will not; nothing is more common than unsuccessful men with talent. Genius will not; the world is full of educated derelicts. Persistence and determination alone are omnipotent."

Kroc's McDonald's initiated many intriguing business concepts, particularly in the field of personnel development. McDonald's managers are screened very carefully. Once selected, they are put through a rigorous training session at "Hamburger University" in Elk Grove, Illinois. There, prospective McDonald's executives are taught the intricacies of managing a successful restaurant. The key concept is Q.S.C.—Quality, Service, Cleanliness.

This intensive personnel-training philosophy proved effective. By 1983 McDonald's had grown to a $3 billion company in sales, with 7,778 restaurants in 30 countries. Ray Kroc had amassed a net worth of $1 billion.

Kroc had other interests besides his company. In 1974 he bought the San Diego Padres for $10 million. He and his second wife, Joan, were very active in the study and prevention of alcoholism. He was also elected to *Fortune* magazine's Business Hall of Fame and received the Horatio Alger Award and an honorary doctorate from Dartmouth. At his death, on January 19, 1984, his estate was worth over $500 million.

MCDONALD'S GOES THROUGH SOME BIG CHANGES

Since Kroc's passing, McDonald's has rolled with the punches landed on it by other burger chains by become increasingly innovative. Burger King, in particular, made inroads on McDonald's market share with its "Have It Your Way" campaign. In response McDonald's has developed its new "Made For You" promotion. McDonald's remains a powerhouse, particularly overseas, where it pulls in over half of its $36 billion in annual sales. But in the U.S., McDonald's has turned to new products and creative marketing to improve its growth, which averaged only 1% for the last four years (as opposed to the 4% average for its competitors, Burger King, Wendy's and Jack-In-The-Box) [*Forbes* "Beyond Burgers" by Bruce Ubin, Nov. 1, 1999]. CEO Jack Greeberg is determined to regain market share by introducing new products. After all, after 44 years as one of the strongest growth companies in the U.S., McDonald's has reached market saturation. Four years ago McDonald's opened about 1000 franchise stores a year; in 2000 it's expected to only open 150.

Greenberg's response has been to allow local franchises more flexibility than they've ever had. As *Forbes* reported, the Midwest franchises came up with the McBrat, which was a huge hit in Wisconsin and Minnesota. Greenberg's insight is that Kroc's system works and works beautifully, so why not apply it to a more diverse range of products? "We owe it to ourselves," James Cantalupo, McDonald's vice chairman, told Ubin, "to see how we can apply those other concepts globally."

Through relentless determination, Kroc took a relatively simple concept (the production of uniform hamburgers) and evolved it into an internally recognized symbol of American free enterprise. Now that his company's almost as huge as Coca Cola, it'll be up to the management he left behind to create a McDonald's for the millennium.

MORE ABOUT RAY KROC

Company Web Site: www.mcdonalds.com

Grinding It Out: The Making of McDonald's by Ray Kroc, St. Martin's Press, 1990

McDonald's: Behind The Arches by John Love, Bantam 1995

Spike Lee

40 ACRES AND A MULE: THE ARTIST AS ENTREPRENEUR

Filmmaker and entrepreneur Spike Lee's exciting career smashes the notion that a creative artist can't also be a shrewd businessperson. Lee has let his enterprising spirit and his belief that African-Americans should start their own businesses lead him into highly successful retail ventures. His controversial movies, meanwhile, have won awards and audiences worldwide.

"We've got to start grooming people to own businesses. That's the only way. Then you can start doing what you want: Keep the money in the community, provide jobs for the people."

Shelton Jackson Lee was born on March 20, 1957 in Atlanta, Georgia, and nicknamed "Spike" by his mother, Jacquelyn. She taught art and literature. Spike's father Bill was a respected jazz bassist and composer. Spike was their first child: a sister, Joie, and three brothers, David, Cinque, and Chris, followed.

After Spike was born, the family moved to Chicago and then to Fort Greene, Brooklyn, in New York City in 1959. As electric guitars and basses began to dominate music in the sixties, Bill Lee's career declined, since he played acoustic bass. The family was supported primarily by Jacquelyn Lee's teaching job at a Brooklyn high school.

A CULTURALLY RICH CHILDHOOD

What the family may have sometimes lacked in money was offset by its rich cultural life. Through his mother, Lee was exposed to plays, museums and art galleries. His father brought him to Manhattan jazz clubs — introducing Lee to the world he would explore in the film "Mo' Better Blues."

After graduating in 1978 from a progressive Brooklyn high school, Lee followed the path of his father and grandfather to Morehouse College in Atlanta, Georgia. The student body and faculty at Morehouse were comprised primarily of African Americans, and Lee found the experience of being immersed in a self-sufficient black community very inspiring. He majored in mass communications and spent his spare time as a disc jockey for a local jazz station and writing for the school paper. He also bought a Super-8 camera and made a couple of short films.

Hooked on film, Lee went to Burbank, California, after graduating from Morehouse in 1979, to work for a summer at Columbia Pictures. That fall he came home to New York and entered New York University's Institute of Film and Television to earn a master's degree in filmmaking.

LEE'S FIRST CONTROVERSY

Lee was one of only a few African Americans at the school and it wasn't long before his first project—a ten-minute film titled "The Answer"—stirred up controversy. Lee's film pointed out the racism in the silent film classic "The Birth of a Nation" that is studied in film classes. His teachers were not pleased, and Lee was almost dismissed from the school.

It was at NYU that Lee met cinematographer Ernest Dickerson, whose richly colored photography has since become a signature of each of Lee's films. As the person who actually operates the cameras, the cinematographer is responsible for transferring the director's vision to film.

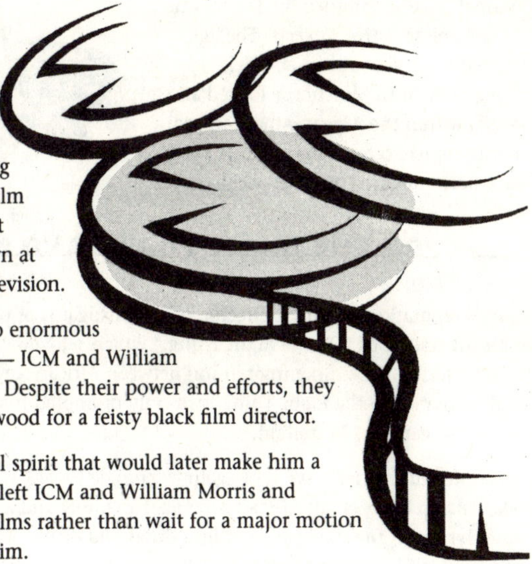

For his master's project, Lee—with Dickerson filming—made the film "Joe's Bed-Stuy Barbershop: We Cut Heads." Lee was already developing his unique mix of wisecracking humor and realness and the film was a hit. It received a student Academy Award and was shown at film festivals and on public television.

All this acclaim prompted two enormous and powerful talent agencies — ICM and William Morris — to sign Lee in 1982. Despite their power and efforts, they could not find work in Hollywood for a feisty black film director.

Displaying the entrepreneurial spirit that would later make him a success in the retail field, Lee left ICM and William Morris and decided to produce his own films rather than wait for a major motion picture company to finance him.

His first effort failed due to a dispute with the Screen Actors Guild. Lee had asked the actors' union to allow him to use nonunion actors — who would be cheaper — in his film. The Screen Actors Guild refused, even though it often did grant such waivers to small films.

"SHE'S GOTTA HAVE IT" BREAKS THROUGH

Even though Lee had spent around $40,000 on this film before failing to be able to complete it, he refused to be discouraged from his goal of producing and directing his own films. For his next film, he wrote a script that could be done cheaply with very few actors. This film, "She's Gotta Have It," was shot in twelve days in the summer of 1985 on a shoestring budget of $175,000. Many times during the filming Lee ran out of money and had to ask friends and family for help.

The movie was an astounding success, earning $1.8 million in its first week and eventually earning over $7 million. It won the prestigious Cannes Film Festival award for best new film and became the first movie by an independent black filmmaker to be distributed internationally by a major distributor since 1971.

The distributor, Island Pictures, offered Lee $4 million to make his next film, "School Daze," but backed out of the deal in 1987 when it looked like the film was going over budget. Undaunted, Lee spent two days on the phone and worked out a $6 million deal with Columbia pictures.

"School Daze" continued the Lee tradition of tackling sensitive subjects. The light-hearted musical about an all-black college similar to Morehouse looked at racism within the African-American community, where often lighter-skinned people have been preferred over dark-skinned people.

"DO THE RIGHT THING" AND "JUNGLE FEVER"

Spike's reputation as both a director and an instigator of public debate was cemented with the release of "Do the Right Thing," which set New York City on its ear with its exploration of the simmering tension between African Americans and Italian Americans in Brooklyn. "Do the Right Thing" not only prompted news editorials around the country, it also earned $28 million.

Spike probed this sensitive spot again in "Jungle Fever," which mixed the story of a love relationship between an African-American architect and a secretary from Bensonhurst, Brooklyn, with the tragic descent into drugs and death of the architect's brother. Spike had trouble filming on location in Bensonhurst because residents were afraid to rent out their homes or shops. Filming was halted one night by bomb threats, and a florist shop in a nearby neighborhood that was used as a location was vandalized.

MERCHANDISING

Lee had begun selling merchandise connected with his films after the success of "She's Gotta Have It" through an informal mail-order operation. After "Do the Right Thing," Lee's studio, 40 Acres and a Mule, was selling $50,000 a month worth of film T-shirts and Brooklyn Dodgers baseball caps. (The studio was named for a promise that slaves freed after the Civil War would each receive forty acres to farm and a mule—the promise was never kept.)

This encouraged Lee to open a store called Spike's Joint in a renovated brownstone near the studio in Fort Greene a few blocks from where Lee was raised. Spike's Joint provided fans with T-shirts, caps, books, and posters, along with Dodger caps and banners.

Meanwhile, Lee's profile rose with the popular commercials he shot in 1988 for Nike Inc.'s Air Jordan sneakers featuring basketball star Michael Jordan. Lee appeared in the Nike commercials as the fast-talking Mars Blackmon, the character he played in "She's Gotta Have It." The president of a black ad agency noted in *Business Week* that Lee is the first African-American ad pitchman whose appeal is based on a celebration of his color.

SPIKE LEE THE ENTREPRENEUR

Lee shrewdly realized that his talent and flair for controversy, as well as his TV commercial appearances, made him a pop culture icon who could branch out from film into fashion and music. He opened his own record company, 40 Acres and a Mule Musicworks, and began developing a line of sportswear, noting in *Women's Wear Daily* that "Anytime you're in business and you can unify things, it gives you that much more power."

Lee's style-setting ability was confirmed by the incredible popularity of the "X" cap he designed to promote the film Malcom X in 1991. By the time the film was being made, imitation caps were available all over the country. Lee realized that he had to protect and develop his fashion business.

Lee hired Jeffrey Tweedy, the former East Coast regional manager for Ralph Lauren Womenswear, to help him with "the transition from the mom & pop [store] to a money-making machine" — as Spike said in an interview with a menswear magazine.

In June 1992, Macy's opened a Spike's Joint in its Manhattan store. This was soon followed by Spike's Joints in 16 other Macy's stores. In August, Lee opened a Spike's Joint on trendy Melrose Avenue in Los Angeles. He began negotiating a licensing deal with Cedars American Inc., a subsidiary of Cedars Japan, to open five Spike's Joint stores in Japan. Lee made Tweedy vice president of 40 Acres and a Mule Products, which includes Spike's Joint shops and Spike's Joint Products, which develops the three sportswear lines. The least expensive line is called Spike's Joint, and includes T-shirts, shorts, and baseball shirts. The Joints By Spike Lee collection includes blazers, jeans, and woven shirts. A higher-priced line called 40 Acres and a Mule is being designed. Lee even established the 40 Acres and a Mule Film Institute at Brooklyn's Long Island University to teach would-be directors the business of filmmaking.

Somewhere in the midst of all this activity, Lee found time to write six books about his films, as well as *Best Seat In The House: A Basketball Memoir*, which is about his passion for basketball in general, and the New York Knicks in particular. In 1993 he married corporate attorney Tonya Lewis; they have a daughter, Satchel, and a son, Jackson.

In 1999, Lee released his first documentary, "Four Little Girls," about the bombing of a black church in Birmingham,

Alabama, in 1963 that killed four black girls. It's a story that Lee has wanted to tell on film since 1983, but he was unable to get the youngest girl's father to agree until recently. [*ABC News Online, Mr. Showbiz Interview* by Gary Susman, Nov. 1999].

ENTREPRENEURSHIP 3D POWER

Lee's not done creating new businesses, however. Shortly after wrapping "Four Little Girls" he formed his own ad agency, Spike/DDB. Lee equates owning a business with freedom and power. He noted in the *WWD* interview that "For so long, we African-American people have been taught to work for other people and not to build our own businesses."

Despite his desire to put into action Malcom X's principle of putting African-American capital to work in the community, Lee has had trouble finding enough African-American vendors for his apparel business. As he said in *Esquire* in a 1991 interview: "We've got to start grooming people to own businesses. That's the only way. Then you can start doing what you want: Keep the money in the community, provide jobs for the people."

MORE ABOUT SPIKE LEE

Spike Lee: By Any Means Necessary by Jim Haskins, Walker and Co., 1997

Best Seat In The House: A Basketball Memoir by Spike Lee, Ralph Wiley, Three Rivers, 1998

Anita Roddick

THE BODY SHOP, INC.: BUSINESS AS A FORCE FOR SOCIAL CHANGE

Anita Roddick and her husband Gordon didn't expect The Body Shop body care company to set the cosmetics industry on its ear, be a force for social change, and make loads of money — but it has. Roddick just wanted to run a small shop to support her and her two children while Gordon fulfilled his dream of riding horseback from Buenos Aires, Argentina, to New York.

*"One of the **greatest successes** of entrepreneurship is to find out what is wanted."*

Roddick opened her first store in Brighton, England, in 1976 with no knowledge of business other than the idea that business is simply trading. She later said: "We [entrepreneurs] are no more or less than simply traders, and trade, be it in a market stall or a shop, is simply a place where buyer and seller come together."

Roddick didn't think of herself as an entrepreneur yet, but she instinctively pinpointed a consumer need by thinking about something that annoyed her—the cosmetics business.

MOTIVATED BY IRRITATION

"My motivation for going into the cosmetics business was irritation: I was annoyed by the fact that you couldn't buy small sizes of everyday cosmetics... I also recognized that a lot of the money I was paying for a product was being spent on fancy packaging which I didn't want," Roddick wrote in her biography, *Body And Soul: Profits With Principles*.

Where most people see irritations, entrepreneurs see opportunities. Roddick decided to sell cosmetics made from natural ingredients in five different sizes of cheap plastic containers.

By doing so, Roddick pricked the cosmetics industry's bubble and set the foundation for her own massive success. As she has said: "One of the greatest successes of entrepreneurship is to find out what is wanted."

Roddick chose her business the old-fashioned way: find a consumer need and fill it with a reasonably priced product. The cosmetics industry, in contrast, was in the business of creating false needs in women's minds and filling them. To do so required tons of advertising and marketing.

It also required false pricing. First, the consumer had to pay for the fancy packaging and expensive ads. Second, the consumer paid for the image of the product. Cosmetics executives could charge extravagant prices for their perfumes and skin-care lotions because their ads made extravagant claims for the results women could expect from the products. Price became part of the image for many products. One perfume, for example, was marketed as the most expensive perfume in the world.

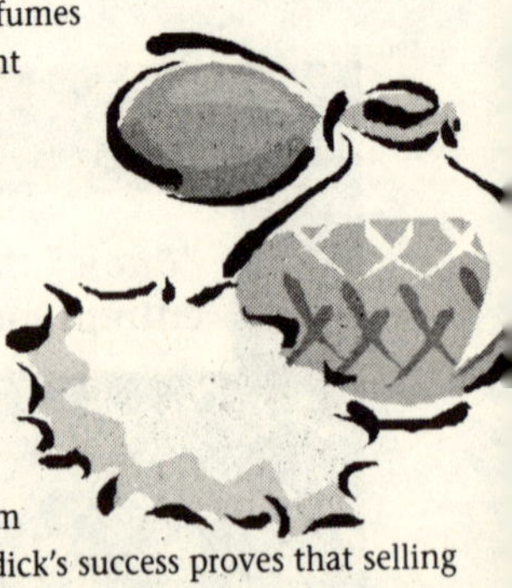

Roddick believed that what the cosmetics houses were doing was wrong. As she said in her book: "It is immoral to deceive a customer by making miracle claims for a product. It is immoral to use a photograph of a glowing sixteen-year-old to sell a cream aimed at preventing wrinkles in a forty-year-old." Roddick's success proves that selling an honest product honestly is the best business strategy of all.

AN ENGLISH CHILDHOOD

During her childhood, Roddick developed the work ethic, love of theatrics, trust in her instincts, and passion for social justice that later helped her become so successful.

Her parents, Donny and Gilda Perella, were Italians who had immigrated to the small English seaside town of Littlehampton. They ran the Clifton Cafe, which opened at 5 a.m. every morning to provide breakfast for the local fisherman. It stayed open each day until there were no more customers coming in for fish and chips.

Roddick was born in 1942, the third of four children. All the children worked in the cafe after school and on weekends. At home the family slept in one room of their apartment, and rented out the other bedroom to make money.

HER REAL FATHER

When Roddick was eight, her mother divorced Donny Perella and married his cousin Henry. This made Roddick very happy because for some reason she had always felt closer to her Uncle Henry than to her father. Ten years later she found out that her instincts had been right when her mother told her that Henry—not Donny—was actually her father.

Gilda's family had arranged for her to marry Donny, but a few months before the wedding she fell in love with his cousin Henry. As a dutiful Italian daughter, though, Gilda went through with the wedding to Donny. She never forgot Henry and wrote to him. A few years later he moved to Littlehampton and they began a secret love affair that resulted in Roddick and her brother Bruno, who were raised as Donny's children.

Sadly, Henry died of tuberculosis only eighteen months after he and Gilda were finally married. Before he died, though, he bought the Clifton Cafe from Donny and transformed it into an American-style diner. Pinball machines, a colorful jukebox, and an American menu soon turned the cafe into a popular hang-out. This was Roddick's first lesson in using atmosphere and excitement to draw customers.

After Henry's death, the children and Gilda Perella had to work hard to maintain the cafe and survive. During this tough time, Roddick came across a book about the Holocaust. The photographs of people suffering from starvation and torture at a Nazi concentration camp horrified her and awakened her social conscience. "After that I would drive my mother mad pestering her for subscriptions to whatever good cause I might have stumbled across," she wrote in her autobiography.

Books and learning became important outlets for Anita's energy and curiosity. When she finished high school she went to college to become a school teacher.

RODDICK DISCOVERS TRAVEL

Roddick enjoyed teaching, but a three-month trip to study children on an Israeli kibbutz unearthed an even greater love of travel. After she returned from Israel she went to Paris to spend a few weeks before beginning a new teaching job, but realized she didn't want to go back to England. She stayed in Paris for almost a year working and exploring the city's culture. She returned to England to teach briefly before she went to Geneva to work for the United Nations.

Roddick took her savings from this job and set off alone for Tahiti, New Hebrides, New Caledonia and Australia—where she stayed briefly before traveling through Reunion, Madagascar, and Mauritius to South Africa.

During her travels, Roddick loved meeting local people and learning their customs. She ate native food and tried native beauty rituals. In Tahiti, for instance, she noticed that despite the harsh drying sun, all the woman had beautiful soft skin because they rubbed cocoa butter onto it. Years later, The Body Shop would sell "body butter" based on this ancient skin-care concept.

LEARNING BUSINESS LESSONS FROM EXPERIENCE

When she ran out of money, Roddick returned to Littlehampton. Her mother introduced her to a quiet young man named Gordon Roddick who had also done a lot of traveling. Instincts must run strong in the Perella women because within four days, Roddick and Gordon moved in together and soon started a family.

The unmarried couple had a baby girl named Justine in August 1969. They got married on a whim in Reno, Nevada, during a visit to the United States while Roddick was pregnant with their second daughter, Samantha, and have been together ever since.

The Roddicks turned a rundown hotel in Littlehampton into a bed-and-breakfast in the summer of 1971 and soon learned a business lesson—don't be afraid to admit you've made a mistake. The inn did well during the summer months when tourists were visiting the seaside, but emptied out in the fall. The Roddicks filled the empty rooms with permanent residents instead of bed-and-breakfast visitors.

Another lesson was learned when they opened a health food restaurant. Littlehampton residents thought the food was weird. The Roddicks realized that you can't impose your will on your customers. They switched to an American-style hamburger restaurant that became very popular.

Running a hotel and a restaurant and caring for two young children exhausted the young couple, however, so they closed the restaurant. Gordon wanted to fulfill his lifelong ambition of trekking across South America on horseback and he and Roddick talked a lot about what she could do to support herself and the children while he was away. They decided to open a shop selling natural cosmetics called The Body Shop.

HOW NOT TO GET A BANK LOAN

To obtain money to open the shop Roddick went to see a bank manager to ask for a loan using the hotel as collateral. She figured that since the bank could always take away the hotel if the loan was not paid back, the bank manager would give her the loan.

She went to see him with her two small children, wearing a Bob Dylan T-shirt and talking excitedly about all the natural ingredients she had discovered on her travels. The bank manager refused to give her the loan.

In those days, banks were unwilling to lend money to women to start businesses. It was easier for women to get money to renovate their kitchens than to start a potentially profitable business, Roddick has said.

A week later she and her husband returned to see the same bank manager. They wore suits and carried a written business plan and Gordon did the talking. This time the loan was approved.

STYLE FROM NECESSITY

With the loan money Roddick rented a shop for six months in Brighton, a town close to Littlehampton but more fashionable and hip. Some of the things she did at first out of necessity became a permanent part of The Body Shop's style.

She couldn't afford to buy lots of bottles at first, so she told customers to bring theirs back for refills — this started recycling. Similarly, Roddick couldn't afford to put perfume in each of her different products, so she filled a tray with little bottles of perfume essences and let the customers put their own perfume in their purchases. This was fun for the customers and became a popular Body Shop practice.

Since some of the creams and lotions were unusual, Roddick and friends hand wrote cards for each product explaining what the ingredients were and how they worked. Offering customers honest information instead of hype became a fundamental Body Shop philosophy.

A week before the shop was to open, Roddick received a letter from a lawyer for two nearby funeral parlors threatening to sue her unless she changed the name of the shop. Roddick called a local newspaper, which wrote up a big article about the threat that scared off the lawyers and got The Body Shop tons of free publicity.

The Body Shop has never paid for product advertising. Roddick estimates the company gains roughly £$32 million ($96 million) per year in free publicity from its various campaigns against social and environmental problems. Clearly, doing the "right thing" is in the best interest of the business.

VENTURE CAPITAL FROM A FRIEND

By the summer of 1976 Roddick wanted to open another shop. The bank refused to lend her money to open the new shop because she had only been in business for a few months so Roddick sold half the business to a friend named Ian McGlinn for £34,000. Today McGlinn's investment is worth over £140 million.

Meanwhile, Gordon came home after one of his horses died in a fall in the Bolivian Andes. He was impressed with the shops and decided to help Roddick expand the business.

By 1978 the Roddicks had helped several people start Body Shops franchise stores in England. The franchisee put up the money to open the shop and the Roddicks provided a license to use the Body Shop name, the products to sell, and their own expert help. Soon franchises opened in other European countries.

The Body Shop's unique products were developing through experience. When the London Marathon race began and many runners complained about sore feet, for example, Roddick had an herbalist develop a Peppermint Foot Lotion. Free samples were handed out along the route of the marathon and the lotion became very popular.

Unlike most cosmetic companies, though, The Body Shop didn't invest lots of money in packaging or advertising, so if a product didn't sell all that was lost was the cost of the ingredients. This gave the Roddicks room to experiment with new products.

FRANCHISING

By 1982, the Roddicks had to move their warehouse and offices to a bigger location and new shops were opening at the rate of two a month all over Europe. The bank was no longer rejecting the Roddicks' requests for financing for different projects. All the franchise stores had the same wonderful smell inside due to the perfume tray, but they were starting to look very different because Roddick and Gordon had never wanted to tell their franchisees what to do.

With success, though, came concern about potential competition. The Roddicks realized that giving each shop a strong identity was very important: it helped customers recognize and remember the business. They convinced the franchisees to make all the shops look very similar.

By 1981 the company was large enough to go public (have its stock sold on the British stock market). The Roddicks wanted to sell stock in the company to raise money to make the business more financially secure. They also liked the idea of making their employees shareholders so they would feel like owners of the business.

Gordon didn't want to go public, though, until the business was ready. He spent two years setting up a good accounting system and working on various legal and financial problems with stockbrokers and advisors.

OVERNIGHT MILLIONAIRES BECOME "ENLIGHTENED CAPITALISTS"

The Body Shop stock went on sale in April of 1984 and quickly rose in price on the stock market the first day until the company was worth £38 million. The Roddicks were millionaires.

Roddick and Gordon went home that night and discussed their future. Suddenly they had power in the business world and they both wanted to use that power wisely. Roddick had already been campaigning against animal testing of cosmetics; now she had the clout to make her voice heard.

She and Gordon decided to use the shops as a force for social change. They call their approach to business "enlightened capitalism." It is based on the idea that what is good for the community and for the world is also good for business. As Roddick has said, "You have to put back in as much as you take out — the spirit of the company is as important as the products."

First, in 1985, they paid for Greenpeace, an environmental group, to put up posters protesting the dumping of hazardous waste into the North Sea. Customers could join Greenpeace at Body Shop stores.

The next year The Body Shop used some of its stores to protest the slaughter of sperm whales for their oil. Unlike many cosmetics stores, The Body Shop used jojoba oil, a desert plant wax, instead of sperm oil in its products. Greenpeace designed posters and leaflets for the stores.

The Body Shop worked next with Friends of the Earth on campaigns against acid rain and on dangers to the ozone layer from aerosol sprays. During these campaigns the Roddicks learned to keep the message clear and provide plenty of easy-to-understand information to Body Shop employees and customers.

ATTRACTING ATTENTION AND CUSTOMERS

The environmental campaigning attracted media attention as well as customers. It also made the employees of the stores happier and more motivated, as their jobs now offered them an opportunity to learn about new things and change the world, not to just sell skin-care products.

Soon The Body Shop was pushing information as well as creams and lotions. Bags — from recycled paper, of course — were printed with information and addresses, and Body Shop trucks had slogans like "If you think education is expensive, try ignorance," painted on them.

Some campaigns have been highly successful. In 1989 the European Community proposed that all cosmetics be tested on animals. More than 5 million people signed The Body Shop's petition against this and the proposal was withdrawn.

THE BODY SHOP FOUNDATION

In 1990, Roddick established The Body Shop Foundation, a non-profit which gathers funds raised by the company's owners, directors, and employees. In 1992 the Foundation created the Brazilian Health Project, which works with Brazilian agencies to support immunization and other medical programs, as well as hospital renovations for 4,000 Indians in 18 Amazon villages [The Body Shop, Inc. press releases].

Children On The Edge, another Body Shop Foundation program, renovates orphanages in Romania and Albania. Since June 1990, hundreds of Body Shop employees have traveled to these countries at their own expense every summer to work with the children.

More recently, a campaign for Amnesty International has resulted in the release of 15 political prisoners due to letters from Body Shop customers. As Roddick said in a speech in New York in 1993: "That is the relevancy of what business should be doing in the marketplace."

TRADE NOT AID

The "Stop the Burning" campaign focused public attention on the destruction of the Brazilian rainforest, which was being burned to create cattle pasture. To further assist the Amazon rainforest tribes, Roddick traveled to Brazil to meet with tribal leaders as part of The Body Shop's "Trade Not Aid" program.

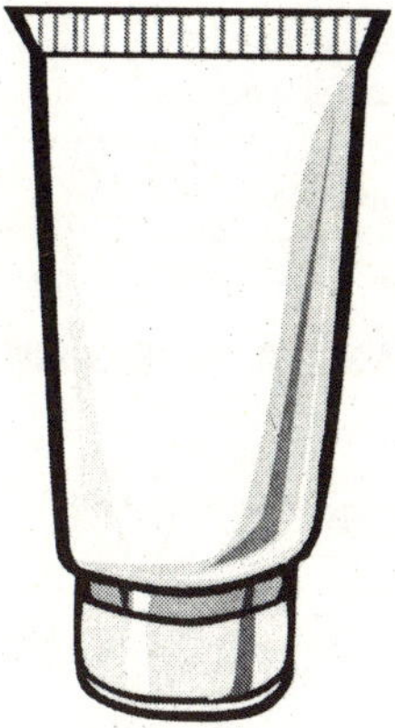

This program stemmed from the Roddicks' belief that the best way to help people in poor countries is to help them establish their own small businesses. "We avoid governments and go straight to the people in the countries," Roddick says.

First, The Body Shop bought wooden foot massage rollers from a boys' town in India. Next, they developed trade with family factories in Nepal that made beautiful paper from a local weed.

Roddick lived in Brazil with the Kayapo Indians exploring how she could start trade with them that would help them and not destroy their culture. The Body Shop now buys brazil nut oil and vegetable dye beads from the tribe and is committed to helping them survive.

Although the Roddicks are deeply committed to using their business to help people and protect the environment, Roddick says,
"I am not rushing around the world as some kind of loony do-gooder; first and foremost I am a trader looking for trade."

THE BODY SHOP IN AMERICA

The Body Shop expanded cautiously into the United States. Many British retailers had failed to succeed in the United States due to the high cost of getting established in the large American market. Yet, the Roddicks had received many letters from Americans who had bought their products in Europe and wanted to find them at home.

The first U.S. Body Shop opened in New York in 1988 and was an instant success. By 1992, 88 more stores were open in the U.S., as The Body Shop fought off competition from other American cosmetics companies launching their own "natural" products.

Today The Body Shop International PLC has 1,500 outlets in 47 countries and over 86 million customers. The company estimates that it sold one of its products every

0.4 seconds in 1997 and 1998. Each store is expected to get involved with a local community project. The store staff is allowed to do volunteer work at the project on company time. Roddick says: "I pay my staff to be active citizens."

As managing director of The Body Shop, Roddick spends about five months a year traveling — looking for new body-care ideas, working on environmental and social causes, and promoting enlightened capitalism. She launched a new consumer magazine, *The Naked Body*, in the UK in the summer 1999.

Roddick suggests that new entrepreneurs ask themselves three questions when trying to choose a business to pursue: 1) What makes you mad? 2) What are you good at? and 3) What separates you from the pack? Answering those questions has created a life for Roddick beyond what she ever imagined for herself when she was a young mother opening her first shop in Brighton.

MORE ABOUT ANITA RODDICK

Company Web Site: www.the-body-shop.com

Anita: The Woman Behind The Body Shop by Jules Older, Charlesbridge Publishing, 1998

Body and Soul: Profits With Principles by Anita Roddick, Russell Miller (out of print)

Russell Simmons

RUSH COMMUNICATIONS, INC.:
MARKETING URBAN CULTURE TO MAINSTREAM USA

Passion is what keeps an entrepreneur going when the going gets tough. Russell Simmons took his passion for rap, music most people thought was just a fad, and turned it into the largest African-American-owned business in the entertainment industry by the time he was 35. Today his company, Rush Communications, Inc., is a diversified multi-media conglomerate that includes a record label, Def Jam Recordings; a management company, Rush Artist Management; the television shows Russell Simmons Television and Russell Simmons' Oneworld Music Beat; a magazine, *Oneworld*; an ad agency, Rush Media Co.; a film company, Def Pictures, and even a clothing company, Phat Fashions.

"We don't make records, music, or television for black people, but for people who consume black culture."

Simmons' personal wealth is estimated at over $80 million. Def Jam Recordings alone earned almost $200 million in revenue in 1998. Some people, including *Salon* writer Jeff Stark in his profile of Simmons (*Salon*, July 6, 1999), are beginning to compare Def Jam's consistent hitmaking and influence to Motown's achievements in its heyday.

Simmons was able to accomplish all this because he never underestimated the consumer. He didn't assume, for instance, that only African Americans would be interested in rap music. He marketed Run DMC, LL Cool J, and other rap artists to both African-American and white audiences.

"The market's come to us, we haven't come to them," Simmons said in an interview in *Worth* magazine in 1992. "We don't make records, music, or television for black people, but for people who consume black culture."

PUSHING HIP-HOP INTO THE MAINSTREAM

Simmons' goal was to sell black culture to anyone who would listen. He used his talent for hype and image-making to push hip hop culture so far into the mainstream that his artists—both African-American and white—sold millions of records. A cover story in *Black Enterprise* magazine in December, 1992, noted that Simmons "has gone beyond selling music and managing artists to marketing the very fabric of black urban culture to mainstream America."

Simmons grew up in a comfortable, middle-class home in Hollis, Queens. His father, Daniel, is a supervisor of attendance in Queens School District 29. His mother, Evelyn, is a painter. His parents encouraged in Russell a respect and passion for the arts.

PROMOTING RAP SHOWS ON CAMPUS

Russell was a student of sociology at the City University of New York when he heard his first rapper—Eddie Cheeba at the Charles Gallery on 125th Street—in 1977. Simmons and his younger brother Joey, who would later become Run of the rap group Run DMC, started promoting rap shows on campus. Simmons named his promotion venture "Rush" after his teenage nickname.

A reporter for *Billboard* named Robert Ford saw the Rush concert promotion stickers Russell and Joey had plastered all over the subway stations in New York and wrote a story about their shows. In 1979 Ford, Simmons, and a friend wrote the song "Christmas Rappin" for rap artist Kurtis Blow, whom Simmons was managing. The song was a club hit, and Mercury Records began distributing the single to record stores around the country.

This was the first rap single to be distributed by a major record company, but rap music was still considered a passing fad by most people...except Russell Simmons. While still in school, he put most of his energy into promoting his records and shows.

SIMMONS AND RUBIN

In 1983 he befriended Rick Rubin, another rap-obsessed student promoter — who was white. In his dark wraparound glasses and black overcoat the long-haired bearded Rubin looked sinister. He had been a heavy metal fan before he discovered rap. Rubin had released a local dance hit by T La Rock and Jazzy Jay called "It's Yours" from his dorm room at New York University. This was one of Simmons's favorite records.

Simmons and Rubin formed Def Jam Records with $5,000.00 and put out a single by an unknown 15-year-old rapper named LL Cool J. While Rubin concentrated on producing the music, Simmons worked on image, getting LL Cool J out of the cowboy boots he liked to wear and into the Kangol hat and sneakers that were to become his trademark. The single sold over 50,000 copies. By the end of the next year Def Jam had sold over 300,000 units of seven different twelve-inch singles.

Their success attracted CBS Records, which offered to help them promote and market four new acts a year. In two years with CBS, Def Jam scored three big hits: the first crossover rap/rock single, "Walk This Way" with Run DMC and Aerosmith, LL Cool J's two-million-seller album, and the Beastie Boys album that went quadruple platinum.

While Rick Rubin concentrated on the music, Simmons started Rush Artist Management to handle and promote Def Jam artists. The fast growth of the partners' business caused problems, however, that eventually drove them apart.

Simmons and Rubin had different musical tastes; Rubin preferred harder-edged music than Simmons did. They also had different goals, which surfaced when they tried to renegotiate their deal with CBS.

SIMMONS CHOOSES CBS MUSCLE

Although 70 percent of the sales for CBS's black-music division were coming from Def Jam artists, Simmons and Rubin still had to struggle with CBS executives over many issues. Rubin wanted to take only a small advance from CBS and keep Def Jam independent. Simmons wanted to break and establish the acts he managed. He wanted to push hip hop into mainstream America, and knew he needed CBS's marketing and promotional muscle to do it.

Rubin and Simmons split their partnership and Rubin left for Los Angeles, where he established Def American Records. Simmons continued to negotiate with CBS, which had been bought by Sony Inc.

Typically, a major label takes the profit from the sales and distribution of an independent label's records and only pays the independent label a royalty. In 1990 Simmons and Sony set up a joint venture that gave Simmons a share of all profits from his artists' records. This was a much better deal than any rap record label had ever obtained before from a major label. The deal also gave Def Jam $3 million per year for its operating costs.

With his record label financially secure, Simmons set his sights on new ways to market the rap phenomenon without watering it down.

Simmons had already dabbled in bringing hip hop to Hollywood, with so-so success. He had co-produced the movie "Krush Groove," which was loosely based on his own life, in 1985, and "Tougher Than Leather," featuring Run DMC, in 1987. Although both movies made some money at the box office, they did not earn Simmons instant respect in Hollywood, as he learned when he tried to produce a movie from the script for "Boyz N the Hood."

Despite his millions, Simmons has never changed his B-boy style of dress or his language, which is often peppered with swear words. He sees this as part of his commitment to street culture.

When Simmons met with Frank Price, the head of Columbia Pictures, to discuss producing "Boyz N the Hood," however, Price was reportedly turned off by Simmons' dress and language enough to not want to work with him. Columbia made the movie — which became a smash hit — without Simmons.

DEF COMEDY JAM ON HBO

After this, Simmons turned his attention to television, as he had once again noticed an exciting subculture that no one else was promoting. On his trips out almost every night to check out new musical talent, Simmons noticed how many discos and rap clubs had comedy nights that were always sold out.

Late in 1991, Simmons showed his talent for choosing not only good artists but good partners when he teamed with Hollywood producers Bernie Brillstein and Brad Grey to produce Russell Simmons' Def Comedy Jam, a series of eight half-hour comedy specials for HBO. The show featured young African-American comics performing raw, uncensored material. It was a huge hit, and HBO asked Simmons, Brillstein and Grey to produce more episodes.

According to HBO research, the show was its most popular late-night comedy program ever, attracting 1.7 million viewers. Approximately two-thirds of the audience were non-African-American.

SIMMONS' ENTERTAINMENT EMPIRE

None of this surprised Simmons, who said in *Entertainment Weekly* that "this is the really hip young black energy that's been driving American popular culture for years." Simmons started yet another company, SLBG Productions, which hunts for new comedy talent.

He also started Russell Simmons Visual Productions (RSVP) with respected film and TV director Stan Lathan to develop a new TV comedy series called "The Johnson Posse." And he did not given up on movies. In 1992 he and Lathan began developing "The Def Adventures of Maximilian Jones" with dePasse Entertainment, and "The Clown Prince," with Tri-Star films.

Simmons also began developing a radio network for the fall of 1993 that will supply a steady stream of hip hop programs to radio stations around the country from New York. He also started a management company to secure endorsements for professional athletes, as well as a modeling agency and a line of hip hop-style clothing called Phat Fashion. His latest venture is Baby Phat swimwear and jewelry lines.

He's actively involved in helping inner-city youth, as well. In 1995 Simmons and his brother Daniel founded The Rush Philanthropic Arts Foundation. The Foundation supports urban programs that expose urban youth to the arts and teaches them not only how to develop their skills but how to be financially successful in the arts. In 1998 Simmons was given the Moet & Chandon Humanitarian Award for his commitment to inner city youth [*World African Network,* "Russell Simmons Wins Humanitarian Award," Dec. 14, 1998].

CHOOSING GOOD PARTNERS AND EMPLOYEES

It's hard to believe that one person could be successful at so many things. Simmons' secret is to choose good partners and employees he can trust to make his creative visions work. When Def Jam started to grow out of control, Simmons hired a 34-year-old African-American corporate lawyer with degrees from Harvard and Yale to tighten up the business. David Harleston set up bookkeeping systems and financial controls.

Harleston was convinced to take the job by Carmen Ashhurst-Watson, the president of Rush Communications. Simmons had hired her earlier to organize his nine companies so they could run smoothly together. One important thing she did was make sure that each separate company had the same fiscal and accounting year.

Simmons's ability to hire very bright and organized people freed him from the day-to-day pressures of running the businesses so he could focus on finding new talent and thinking up new ideas. Many entrepreneurs fail just when they start to become successful because they are afraid to loosen their grip on a growing company. They end up strangling their company because they don't want to let anyone else have any power.

Even in his marriage to Kimora Lee, Simmons managed to find a good partner. Lee's a skilled party organizer who has put together political and social events at their homes (including a party for Hillary Clinton) that have been great publicity for her husband and his company.

Rush Communications flourished because Simmons knows how to find good partners and employees and let them do their jobs. He knows this will help him be true to himself and to hip hop.

MORE ABOUT RUSSELL SIMMONS

Company Web Site: www.defjam.com

Madame C.J. Walker

THE FIRST AFRICAN-AMERICAN MILLIONAIRE

Madame Walker, a pioneer black businesswoman, was born Sarah Breedlove to poor farmers in Louisiana on December 23, 1867. Her parents were ex-slaves and sharecroppers who lived on the Burney plantation in Delta, Louisiana. Breedlove was orphaned in early childhood and reared by her married sister. She was married to a Mr. McWilliams at fourteen "to get a home," as she later said. Despite the hardship and poverty of her early years, she went on to become a millionairess by creating hair-and-skin-care products for black women. In fact, she was the first American self-made woman millionairess.

She "revolutionized the personal habits and appearance of millions of human beings."

(NAACP magazine, 1919)

At age 20 she was widowed and moved to St. Louis where, for 18 years, she supported herself and her daughter, A'Lelia, by working as a washerwoman. Because she recognized her need for formal education, she went to classes in the city's public schools at night.

A dramatic change in her life occurred at the age of 38, when she hit upon a formula for a preparation to enhance the hair of black women. She created it by mixing soaps and ointments in washtubs. In addition, she modified various existing hairdressing techniques. Finally, after experimenting on herself and her family, she arrived at what was to be known as "the Walker Method." It combined a shampoo, a pomade "hair grower," vigorous brushing and the use of heated iron combs. Through this technique, hair became shiny and smooth. In addition, she created a formula especially suited to meet black women's complexion needs. She was convinced of the commercial potential of her products, and after a year of preliminary experiments, she spent two years traveling to promote them.

DOOR-TO-DOOR SALES

In 1906 she moved to Denver, where she married Charles J. Walker, a newspaperman. At first, in Denver, she sold her products door-to-door. This method allowed her to demonstrate them. She also organized a group of "agent-operators" whom she called "hair culturists," "scalp specialists," and "beauty culturists." Walker set herself the tasks of instructing these operators in her methods and the manufacturing of her products.

After about a year, she set up her business and manufacturing headquarter s in Denver. At the same time, she also trained agents in establishing their own businesses. She expanded her enterprise by giving demonstrations and lectures in the South and East. In addition, she set up a thriving mail-order business. These efforts proved so successful that in 1908 she was able to establish a second office in Pittsburgh, which her daughter managed.

In 1910, she moved both offices to Indianapolis. The plant she built there became the center of her operations—the Madame C. J. Walker Laboratories. It was both the place where her products were manufactured and a training school for her agents and beauty culturalists.

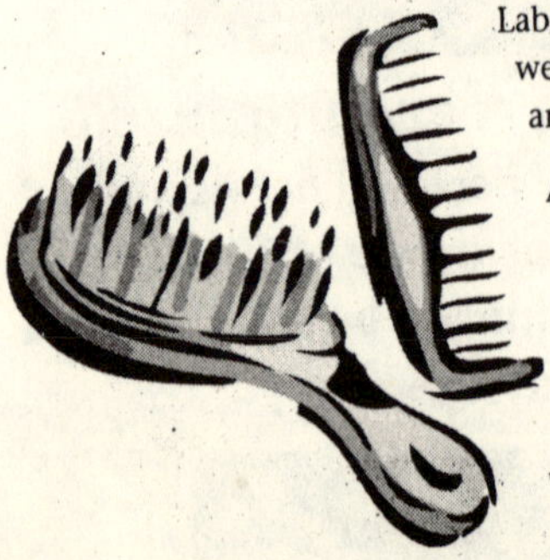

At the peak of her career, she employed about 2,000 agents to sell her products. Dressed in a standardized uniform, they demonstrated and sold 16 different items. An agent could generate more than $50,000 annually. In total, her company provided employment for over 3,000 people. Most of her employees were women who brought the treatments into the

home. (This all occurred before the growth of beauty salons.) These "Walker Agents" became familiar figures throughout the U.S. and the Caribbean.

ORGANIZING HER AGENTS INTO CLUBS

Among her more successful marketing strategies was organizing her agents into "Walker Clubs" that promoted business, social and charitable causes. They set up regular three-day conventions as well. To motivate them, she offered cash prizes to the clubs that did the greatest volume of charitable and education work.

The success of this strategy, combined with her own active instructional tours, made Madame Walker one of the most famous blacks in America. Her fame was carried to Europe when the Walker hair-care system was popularized by the great dancer, Josephine Baker. Parisians became so fascinated by it that a French company produced a similar product they called "Baker-Fix." In the U.S., her work was carried on by other black women.

In 1919, a journalist commented that "The largest and most lucrative business enterprises conducted by black people in America have been initiated by women — namely Madame Walker and Mrs. Malone." Mrs. Malone was a black woman who developed additional beauty systems inspired by Madame Walker's success.

HIGH STANDARDS

Walker required that her agents abide by high standards of hygiene, standards which were later integrated into cosmetology laws. Through frequent communication with her agents, she continuously emphasized "cleanliness and loveliness" as avenues to self-respect and racial advancement. An article in a National Association for the Advancement of Colored People (NAACP) magazine said that Madame Walker "revolutionized the personal habits and appearance of millions of human beings." She was praised by another writer for her teaching the "secret of the enhancement of feminine beauty" to black women.

She was remembered by all who knew her as a person of great simplicity and kindness who was easily approachable. Most important, she was committed to the education and social uplifting of her people. As a consequence of her personnel training, many black women were launched on business careers as agents and beauty culturists. In addition, she was a generous donor to black charities and encouraged her agents to support them, as well. She made the largest single donation to the NAACP's 1918 purchase of Frederick Douglass' house. She also contributed generously to the NAACP's homes for the elderly in St. Louis and Indianapolis, to the poor in Indianapolis and to the Indianapolis YMCA.

Walker was also committed to helping to educate African-Americans. She funded scholarships for both men and women at Tuskegee Institute and to a secondary school for African-Americans founded by her close friend, Charlotte Hawkins Brown.

When she died in 1919 she was the sole owner and president of the Madame C. J. Walker Manufacturing Company. Her estate, valued at over a million dollars, encompassed four houses in New York and Indianapolis and a country estate. Her will designated that two-thirds of her fortune go to educational institutions and charities. After her death, a trust fund created an industrial and mission school in Africa as well as bequests to black orphans.

Mrs. Walker left a rich legacy of black female entrepreneurial leadership that has benefited and inspired women worldwide

MORE ABOUT MADAME C.J. WALKER

Company Web Ste: www.madamecjwalker.com

Madame C.J. Walker: Cosmetics Tycoon by A'Lelia P. Bundles (Walker's great-great-granddaughter), Matilda Publications, New York, 1983

Madame C.J. Walker by Cookie Lommel, Holloway House Publishing, 1993.

Sam Walton

WAL-MART: MASTER OF MOTIVATION

No matter what kind of business you own, motivating yourself and your employees is very important. Sam Walton was a master of motivation. He built Wal-Mart, the largest retailer in the world, from a single five-and-dime store. As of September 1999, there were 1821 Wal-mart stores, 680 Supercenters and 453 Sam's Clubs in the United States. Several hundred stores have been opened internationally, as well. Wal-Mart took in over $139 billion in 1998. Wal-mart is reportedly targeting China as its next market. The company has jumped into the Internet market, as well, with its new online travel agency.

"**Individuals** don't win; **teams** do."

Walton was born in Kingfisher, Oklahoma, in 1918 and lived there until he was five. The Waltons lived in several different towns in Missouri while Sam was growing up. This part of the United States was known as the Dust Bowl during this time, because of a terrible drought that had turned once-rich farmland into dust. The entire country was suffering from the economic effects of the Great Depression, so this was a time of tremendous poverty.

Luckily, Walton's father was a natural negotiator who loved to trade. Once, he traded the family farm in Kingfisher for a farm near Omega, Oklahoma. Another time, Walton recalls in his autobiography (*Sam Walton: Made In America* by Sam Walton with John Huey, Doubleday, New York, 1992), he traded his wristwatch for a hog, to put meat on the family table.

WALTON'S YOUTH BUSINESSES

Walton learned entrepreneurship from his mother, who started a small milk business to help the family make ends meet. Walton began selling magazine subscriptions when he was only eight years old and had paper routes from seventh grade through college. He also raised and sold rabbits and pigeons to help put himself through school. Walton figures he earned about $4,000 to $5,000 a year from his paper routes during college, which was a lot of money to be earning at the end of the Depression. He also waited tables and worked as a lifeguard at a local swimming pool.

After Walton earned a business degree from the University of Missouri he was eager to make something of himself. His first job was with the J.C. Penney store in Des Moines, Iowa. Two things impressed him during his eighteen-month tenure at J.C. Penney — one was meeting James Cash Penney himself, who made a point of visiting every store he could; another was the bonuses J.C. Penney managers earned based on how well their stores performed. Later Walton would apply these motivational strategies to Walton stores.

WALTON BUYS HIS FIRST DEPARTMENT STORE

In 1942, though, Walton was drafted into the Army—just after he had fallen in love with Helen Robson. They married and Walton spent two years in the army. After his stint was over, he was eager to start a department store business with his good friend Tom Bates. He and Bates were all set to buy a department store in St. Louis when Mrs. Walton put her foot down.

According to his autobiography, Walton's wife said, "I'll go with you any place you want so long as you don't ask me to live in a big city. Ten thousand people is enough for me." She was also dead set against partnerships, as her father was a prominent businessman who had seen plenty of partnerships go sour.

Walton had such respect for his wife's business sense and feelings that he agreed. Instead of going into partnership in St. Louis, he bought a Ben Franklin variety store in Newport, Arkansas, a small town of 7,000 people.

THE POWER OF DEEP DISCOUNTING

Once he bought the store, though, he realized that it faced stiff competition from the variety store across the street owned by John Dunham. Walton felt hampered in his efforts to compete by the Ben Franklin franchise, which wanted its stores run a certain way. He wasn't allowed much leeway in pricing or choosing merchandise. Determined to make his store profitable, Walton started cutting his own deals with suppliers rather than relying on the franchise. He also started cutting prices like crazy. One of his first deals was for ladies' panties. Walton had been buying them from Ben Franklin for $2.50 per dozen and selling them at three pair for $1.00. Walton found a supplier who sold him panties at $2.00 per dozen. At that price, Walton could afford to sell them at four for a dollar.

"I found that by pricing [an item] at $1.00 I could sell three times more of it than by pricing it at $1.20. I might make only half the profit per item, but because I was selling three times as many, the overall profit was much greater."

This was the essence of discounting: Cutting your price until you boost your sales to a point where you earn far more at the cheaper retail price than you would have by selling the item at the higher price.

The Ben Franklin franchise was not amused, however. Walton was obligated to buy at least 80 percent of his merchandise from Ben Franklin and he had a hard time meeting that quota. On the other hand, the franchise couldn't deny that all his crazy promotions — a popcorn machine on the sidewalk in front of the store, all kinds of discount specials — were working. Walton took the Ben Franklin store from $72,000 per year in sales under the previous owner to $250,000 per year five years later. It was the number-one Ben Franklin store in the region.

Ironically, Walton was forced at this juncture to sell the store because he had never thought to get an extension on his five-year lease. The landlord was eager to buy the successful store and give it to his son, so he refused to renew Walton's lease. Walton did sell, but to John Dunham, his former competitor.

WALTON TAKES UP FLYING TO MANAGE GROWING WAL-MART BUSINESS

Sick at heart, Walton and his wife decided to take their $50,000 profit from the sale of their store and purchase a new store in a different town. They settled on an old store in Bentonville, Arkansas. Bentonville was, as Helen put it, "just a sad-looking country town" of only 3,000 people. Walton remodeled the store as a self-service variety store; it was only the third in the whole country but people loved digging around in the merchandise and knowing that they were getting an extra-good deal because they were helping themselves.

This time Walton was determined not to build his family's entire life around a single store. He purchased another store in nearby Fayetteville and hired Willard Walker to manage it. He opened a third store with his brother Bud in Kansas City. Suddenly Walton was spending all his time driving between stores. His solution was to scare his family half to death by buying a two-seater airplane.

"Once I took to the air," Walton said, "I caught store fever." He opened more and more Ben Franklin franchise stores with Bud and Helen's two brothers. Despite the success of these variety stores, though, Walton couldn't shake his belief that deep discounting was the way to go. In July, 1962, he finally decided to build his own store, in Rogers, Arkansas. He called it Wal-Mart.

Soon, Walton had three Wal-Marts up and running. He stuck with what he had learned in the variety store business: to emphasize customer service and satisfaction guaranteed. He attracted customers to particular items by placing them on tables at the end of store aisles or by piling them up on "action alley," the big horizontal aisle that runs across a store in front of the checkout counters. Walton was also obsessed with keeping Wal-Mart prices lower than anyone else's. The stores were nothing fancy but, Walton said, Wal-Mart customers, "could be pretty sure they wouldn't find it cheaper anywhere else, and if they didn't like it, they could bring it back."

THE VPI CONTEST

Walton gave his store managers lots of freedom to find good deals to pass on to customers. In fact, he required them to report to him each week on their "Best Selling Item." He also encouraged competition between his stores. One contest was the VPI (volume producing item). The idea was to promote a discounted item in some attention-grabbing fashion so that it would just fly out of the store.

One of the craziest volume promotions was done by Phil Green at the Hot Springs, Arkansas store. A supplier offered him a dollar off every case of laundry detergent if he would buy over three thousand cases. Green bought them and built a giant pyramid of detergent boxes in the store that ran all the way to the ceiling and was almost 100 feet long. Then he ran an ad selling the boxes for $1.99 a box instead of the usual $3.97. Another time Green bought 200 power riding mowers that someone was desperate to sell for $175. Green lined all the mowers up in front of the store, twenty-five in a row, eight rows deep. He sold every one of them at $199 each.

By 1966, Walton knew he had to organize his growing operation more effectively. He hired several experienced merchandisers to help him develop an organization and expansion plan. They decided to build a warehouse near new Wal-Mart offices in Bentonville and computerize their operation. Computers were not common yet in the business world, as they are now, but Walton and his team made a huge investment in sophisticated inventory technology that really paid off once Wal-Mart began expanding around the country.

GOING PUBLIC LEADS TO FURTHER EXPANSION

Walton's next step was to take the company public (sell Wal-Mart stock on the open stock market) to raise capital to pay off debt. The offering took place on Oct. 1, 1970 and since then, Wal-Mart stock has proven to be a very profitable investment. One hundred shares purchased for $1,650 in 1970 would be worth around $3 million today.

Once Wal-Mart was out of debt, Walton was free to pursue his expansion strategy: "to put good-sized discount stores into little one-horse towns which everybody else was ignoring." One of Walton's favorite things to do was to scout for locations from the pilot seat of his little airplane.

In 1970, Wal-Mart had 32 stores and $31 million in sales; by 1980, Walton had opened 276 stores and annual revenue had climbed to $1.2 billion. As Wal-Mart expanded, Walton turned his attention to the issue of how to motivate his increasing number of employees and store managers to keep providing great service and great deals to Wal-Mart customers.

PROFIT SHARING FOR EVERY "ASSOCIATE"

In 1970, Walton introduced profit sharing for Wal-Mart managers. By 1971 he had extended it to every "associate" (as he called his employees) in the company. Using a formula based on profit growth, Wal-Mart contributes a percentage of each associate's wages to a profit-sharing plan, which the associate can take when he or she leaves the company — either in cash or Wal-Mart stock. In 1991, for example, Wal-Mart contributed $125 million to the profit-sharing plan.

The profit-sharing plan has created significant wealth for many Wal-Mart employees, but more importantly, it makes each employee eager to work hard and come up with innovations to improve the profitability of the company. In *Sam Walton: Made in America,* a Wal-Mart truck driver notes that he worked for one large company for thirteen years and left with $700. After working for Wal-Mart for twenty years, he's built up over $700,000 in profit sharing. "When folks ask me how I like working for Wal-Mart," he says, "I tell them about my profit sharing and ask them, 'How do you think I feel about Wal-Mart?'"

Profit-sharing was just one of Walton's motivational innovations. No matter how enormous the company became, his door was open to any employee who needed to talk to him. He constantly visited stores and made people feel that they were an important part of the Wal-Mart team. He encouraged and rewarded healthy competition between his stores.

Walton figured, he said, that "the way management treats the associates is exactly how the associates will then treat the customers. And if the associates treat the customers well, the customers will return again and again."

Walton was also a pioneer regarding the concept of corporate culture. He believed that employees want to feel that their concerns and suggestions are heard by managers. He also wanted to encourage associates to become friends and have fun together. To that end, he started a tradition of Saturday morning meetings that began with the Wal-Mart cheer and went on to include performances by the company's Singing Truck Drivers or persimmon-seed spitting contests.

DANCING THE HULA ON WALL STREET

Walton loved any antic that would motivate people. One time he found himself dancing the hula in a grass skirt on Wall Street after betting his management that they couldn't produce a pretax profit of more than 8 percent—and losing. Doing the hula was nothing, Walton noted, compared to wrestling a bear, which was what one warehouse manager did after he challenged his production team to beat a record.

"This sort of stuff goes on all the time at Wal-Mart," Walton said. "It's part of our culture, and it runs through everything we do... we always have tried to make life as interesting and as unpredictable as we can, and to make Wal-Mart a fun proposition... If you're committed to the Wal-Mart partnership and its core values, the culture encourages you to think up all sorts of ideas that break the mold and fight monotony."

Although he passed away in 1992, Walton's folksy style remains the key to a business that is now worth over $50 billion. Even when *Forbes* named him America's richest man in 1985, Walton preferred pick-up trucks to Rolls Royces, and hunting and fishing to attending celebrity-studded events.

Walton expected his managers and executives to share his aversion to flashy spending, but this wasn't just a billionaire's quirk—it was part of his motivational strategy. In his autobiography, he said, "if American management is going to say to their workers that we're all in this together, they're going to have to stop this foolishness of paying themselves $3 million and $4 million bonuses every year and riding around everywhere in limos and corporate jets like they're so much better than everybody else."

Walton wasn't just paying lip-service to this idea; he put money behind it by spreading Wal-Mart's wealth to its associates via profit-sharing. At the Wal-Mart museum in Bentonville, people there are still sad about his recent passing. Walton's office is reconstructed there, and a copy of the profit-sharing plan hangs on the wall. Although he didn't have a computer in his office, Walton was a great proponent of technology. Wal-Mart's computerized inventory system was ahead of its time and helped Wal-Mart keep its prices so low.

#1 GOOD CORPORATE CITIZEN

Walton also applied his irreverent approach to life and his belief in the importance of motivation to philanthropy. He believed in programs "that require the recipients to work and kick in some of their own money." He had a special passion for trying to improve the American public education system. At the close of his autobiography, Walton wrote, "our country desperately needs a revolution in education. Without a strong educational system, the very free enterprise system that allows a Wal-Mart or an IBM or a Procter & Gamble to appear on the scene and strengthen our nation's economy simply won't work."

Walton would no doubt be pleased with Wal-Mart's ranking as the nation's number one "good corporate citizen" in the *1999 Cone/Roper Cause Related Trends Report*. According to the report, a five-year study found that one in four Americans named Wal-Mart as a good corporate citizen, knocking McDonald's off its #1 pedestal for the first time since 1993. Wal-Mart contributed over $127 million in 1998 to charitable causes and most of the donations and programs are managed by local stores and benefit local communities.

MORE ABOUT SAM WALTON

Company Web Site: www.wal-mart.com

Sam Walton: Made In America: My Story by Sam Walton, John Huey, Bantam Books, 1993

Wal-Mart: A History of Sam Walton's Retail Phenomenon, Twayne Publishing, 1997

Oprah Winfrey

HARPO, INC.

"Dishing the dirt and meddling in other folk's business is what I do best," Oprah Winfrey has said. She has turned her interest in other people's lives into an Emmy-award-winning talk show, The Oprah Winfrey Show. This daytime talk show was launched on 138 TV stations in 1986 by King World Productions and quickly became the most popular talk show in America. Today it is carried by over 200 stations. Winfrey is the third woman in history (after Mary Pickford and Lucille Ball) to own a major studio. In 2000, Winfrey's Harpo Entertainment Group will produce original shows for Oxygen Media's new cable network.

*"I think a lot more **emphasis** has been placed on the **money** than needed to be, because I would have done this job for **free**."*

It was ownership that vaulted Winfrey into the *Forbes* magazine list of the four hundred richest people in America. She was the only performer to make the list in 1995. Her net worth is estimated by *Forbes* at over $400 million. If her show stays on the air at its present popularity, Winfrey is on her way to becoming the first African-American billionaire.

Winfrey made the leap from being just another high-paid performer to a millionaire entrepreneur with the help of her agent, Jeffrey Jacobs. In 1984, she was hosting Chicago's most popular talk show, having actually beaten talk-show king Phil Donahue in the ratings. Her station, ABC affiliate WLS-TV, was paying her $230,000 a year and her agent had negotiated her a four-year contract with annual salary hikes of $30,000.

"PIRANHA IS GOOD"

Winfrey was very excited about her contract—until three different ABC executives mentioned to her how terrific they thought her agent was. This made her wonder whether her agent had really gotten her such a good deal. Why was ABC so pleased with him? She fired the agent and hired Jacobs. "I'd heard Jeff is a piranha," she explained in *Forbes* (Oct. 16, 1995), "I like that. Piranha is good."

Jacobs "took the ceiling off my brain," Winfrey said, by encouraging her to think of herself as an entrepreneur, not just an entertainer. His first move was to retrieve the syndication rights to her show that the previous agent had given up to the local ABC station. Jacobs made a deal that allowed him to sell the show outside the Chicago market as long as ABC stations got first dibs. Next, he brought in King World Productions as distributor of The Oprah Winfrey Show.

WINFREY ACTS IN THE COLOR PURPLE AND BELOVED

Meanwhile, Winfrey's growing popularity received an added boost when producer Quincy Jones cast her in the film adaptation of her favorite book, "The Color Purple" by Alice Walker. Winfrey had only acted once before, in a one-woman theater show, but Jones believed she was a natural actress. Despite her lack of experience, her performance in "The Color Purple" was called "shockingly good" by movie critic Gene Siskel. Her performance was even nominated for an Academy Award. Her success in this movie and subsequent film and television projects turned more people on to her talk show.

Ratings for her show soared. Meanwhile, Winfrey took advantage of the situation by beginning to produce dramatic films and television shows. She signed a multipicture contract with Disney, under which she produced and starred in "Beloved," which was adapted from Toni Morrison's novel by director Jonathan Demme. Although the movie didn't do well at the box office, Winfrey's performance was critically acclaimed once again.

Winfrey's show earned $115 million in revenue during its first two seasons. The show's success gave Winfrey and Jacobs the clout to bring WLS back to the negotiating table and demand that ownership of the show be turned over to Winfrey. Winfrey started her own production company, Harpo (Oprah spelled backwards). In 1994, for example, The Oprah Winfrey Show grossed $196 million. After deducting production costs, Jacobs' ten percent cut (roughly $10 million last year), and other expenses, Winfrey earned about $74 million in pre-tax income from the show.

WINFREY'S BUSINESS CLOUT

King World is now so dependent on her show that a rumor printed in *The Wall Street Journal* that Winfrey was considering quitting her show actually caused the distributor's stock price to fall. As a result, Winfrey was able to negotiate a very favorable five-year deal that will pay her a three to five percent increase in her cut of the distributor's earnings from her show every year. *Forbes* has estimated that her production company's cash flow from the deal over the next five years will be at least $400 million. Every year she will also receive options on 250,000 of King World shares. She already has 1.5 million shares under option—worth $30 million.

In addition, Winfrey's Harpo Studio signed a deal in 1995 with ABC to produce six made-for-TV movies over the next three years. Winfrey is interested in producing sensitive films, videos, and television movies on topics she thinks are important to society.

Winfrey already has a reputation for a frank, caring approach to societal problems. Her show is consistently praised for discussing painful topics—such as racism and childhood sexual abuse— without exploiting them for their shock value to the degree that some other talk shows do.

Of course, Winfrey does plenty of shows that are pure entertainment. She has interviewed Elizabeth Taylor, Julia Roberts, and many other movie stars. Musical guests on her show have ranged from Diana Ross to Michael Bolton.

A CHILDHOOD TALENT FOR PUBLIC SPEAKING

Winfrey has come a long way from the farm in Kosciusko, Mississippi, where she was born in 1954 to unmarried parents who had separated. She was raised by her grandmother, who taught her to read by the time she was only two and a half. The bright little girl skipped kindergarten and, after first grade, was promoted to third grade.

When she was six years old, Winfrey was sent north to live with her mother and two half brothers in Milwaukee's inner city. She missed playing with the farm animals so much that she kept cockroaches in a jar as pets. The African-American community in Milwaukee had strong churches and social groups, and it was here that Winfrey developed her talent for public speaking. She was often invited to recite poetry at church teas and other public events. At age twelve, during a visit to her father in Nashville, she was paid $500 for giving a speech at a church. She told her father that evening that she knew what she wanted to do when she grew up—be "paid to talk."

Back in Milwaukee, however, Winfrey was experiencing some things that she wouldn't talk about for many years. Her mother was having a hard time making enough money to support the family and was often away working. Several men her mother trusted sexually abused Winfrey starting when she was only nine years old.

Confused, angry, and afraid to talk about the abuse, Winfrey started behaving badly. She ran away from home and stole money from her mother's purse. Her frustrated mother finally decided to send her to Nashville to live with her father and his wife.

A SAFE ENVIRONMENT HELPS WINFREY FLOURISH

Luckily, Winfrey's father was a strict, caring man who provided her with a safe environment. She soon began to flourish in school again, especially in drama and debate. When Winfrey was sixteen she won a speaking contest that awarded her a full scholarship to Tennessee State University. While still in high school she was hired by a local radio station to read newscasts after school.

During her freshman year at Tennessee State, Winfrey won two beauty pageants, becoming Miss Black Nashville and Miss Tennessee. She was a contestant in 1971 in the Miss Black America Pageant. All this exposure, combined with her academic excellence, led the local CBS television station to offer her a position as Nashville's first African-American woman to co-anchor the evening news. She was still living with her father and had a midnight curfew.

After graduating, Winfrey wanted to live on her own, so she took a job with WJZ-TV in Baltimore, Maryland. She wasn't prepared, however, for the pressure that the station put on her to change her looks. The assistant news director actually told her: "Your hair's too thick, your nose is too wide, and your chin's too big." He sent her to a New York hair salon that gave her a botched permanent that left her completely bald. On camera she had to cover her head with her scarf until her hair grew back. The humiliation and pressure prompted her to seek comfort in food, beginning her long battle with a weight problem.

DISCOVERING TALK TV

In 1977, the station switched her from her news anchor job to co-hosting a morning talk show with Richard Sher called "Baltimore Is Talking." After her first day on the job, she said: "This is what I was born to do. This is like breathing."

Winfrey spent seven years doing shows with Sher that foreshadowed The Oprah Winfrey Show. The topics of the Baltimore show ranged from divorce to Siamese twins. In Baltimore, their show got better ratings than Phil Donahue's popular show.

In 1984, Winfrey moved to Chicago to take over a dull morning show called A.M. Chicago, that always got the worst ratings in its time slots. Her first move was to change the shows topics from lightweight "women's topics " like cooking and makeup to more topical and controversial subjects. This had been Donahue's successful strategy and it worked for Winfrey, too. Within one month she was even with Donahue in the ratings; by three months she was ahead of him and the show had been renamed The Oprah Winfrey Show.

Another thing that made her show so popular was her natural, friendly style. After conducting an awkward interview with actor Tom Selleck, Winfrey asked the station management to let her throw away scripts and cue cards and just talk with her interview subjects. Winfrey's intelligence and years of public speaking enabled her to think on her feet in front of a camera. She quickly developed a reputation for being unafraid to ask frank questions and to express her opinions and emotions.

Winfrey was also unafraid to behave "like a woman." She was spontaneous, unpredictable, and sympathetic. When interviewing someone about an upsetting topic, she often took the person's hand to help him or her get through a difficult discussion. She was open about her struggle with her weight, and about her childhood sexual abuse.

Her unorthodox style was very popular with her daytime viewers. Winfrey's shows varied from comical to serious, depending on the day's topic. One day she might be interviewing a panel of supermodels, the next discussing how parents can prevent their children from being kidnapped.

COMMITMENT TO SOCIAL AND POLITICAL ISSUES

Her commitment to social and political issues has always been strong, however. As early as 1987, Winfrey launched a yearlong anti-drug campaign with WLS-TV and the *Chicago Sun-Times*. She has done many shows exploring racism in America, including one show that was taped before an all-white audience in Forsyth County, Georgia, where no African-Americans have lived since 1912.

Winfrey is acutely aware of the influence television wields. She believes in trying to exercise that influence responsibly. When asked by columnist Liz Smith if she would ever consider going into politics, Winfrey answered, "No. I think I could have a great influence in politics... But I think that what I do every day has far more impact." (*Good Housekeeping*, Oct. 1995). As for her decision to reject the scandal route and turning her show toward more positive topics, Winfrey said, "I see my TV show as a great forum for teaching. It's the biggest classroom you could ever imagine."

Winfrey enjoys the trappings of success—a designer wardrobe and expensive homes—but she gives a great deal of her time and money to charity. She has worked with the Little Sisters program at Chicago's Cabrini-Green housing projects for years and has recently started a new program to help move one hundred families out of housing projects that will cost her millions of dollars. She has made huge grants to educational institutions, including her college, Tennessee State University, and her foundation, Family For Better Lives. She's even co-taught a class at Northwestern University's Kellogg Graduate School of Management called "The Dynamics of Leadership" with her fiance, Stedman Graham.

Winfrey sees her partnership with Oxygen Media as an extension of her commitment to both women and more positive TV. Oxygen, which is currently a web-site, plans to debut as a 24-hour/day cable network Feb 2, 2000. Winfrey will be producing two shows, initially. She's also developing a magazine for Hearst Magazines that is expected to hit newsstands in March of 2000. The magazine, as yet unnamed, will target women in their thirties.

Winfrey's contract for the "Oprah Winfrey Show" expires in 2002, so perhaps Winfrey is positioning herself to leave the talk show world. As she told *Newsweek*, "Part of the reason that I wanted to participate in [Oxygen] is so I wouldn't have to give up my voice, and that has been something so important to me as a descendant of slaves who had no voice. I want to maintain that. Oxygen gives me that voice." [*Newsweek*, "Talk Show: 'Oxygen Gives me That Voice'", Nov. 15, 1999 interview with Lynette Clemetson]

MORE ABOUT OPRAH WINFREY

Company Website: www.oprah.com

Oprah by Judeth Mahoney Pasternak, Metro Books, Sept. 1999

The Uncommon Wisdom of Oprah Winfrey: A Portrait In Her Own Words by Oprah Winfrey and Bill Adler (editor), Citadel Publishing, July 1999

Steve Wozniak & Steve Jobs

APPLE COMPUTERS

"Never **trust** a computer you can't throw out the window." (Steve Wozniak)

"We started off with a very idealistic perspective — that doing something with the **highest quality**, doing it right the first time, would really be cheaper than having to go back and do it again." (Steve Jobs)

Very few recent business success stories rival that of Apple Computer, which was started in a garage by two computer nerds in their early twenties. Founded in Cupertino, California, in 1976, by 1984 Apple had sales of $1.5 billion and was number 234 on the Fortune 500 list of America's top companies. After Steve Jobs left the company in 1985, Apple went into decline as the popularity of its operating system was knocked out by the growing dominance of Microsoft's MS-DOS system. Jobs' return in 1996 marked the end of Apple's decline and he has since turned the company around with the introduction of the iMAC and the PowerMac G3. Sales in 1998 were almost $6 billion.

Apple changed computers from big scary machines found in universities and military bases to cute, user-friendly boxes that ordinary people weren't afraid to bring home. Jobs and Wozniak defined an entire industry by uncovering the large market for the personal home computer. And by taking on IBM, the fledgling company gave courage to many struggling entrepreneurs who were up against corporate Goliaths.

The two creators of Apple Computer, though personally as different as night and day, became one of the most successful entrepreneurial teams in the history of American business. Steven Jobs has become one of the most famous businessmen in the world. Much less, however, is known about the older, and perhaps the most important, Apple partner.

"THE WOZ"

Stephen Wozniak was born on August 11, 1950 in Sunnyvale, California, a small town in what was to become the famous Silicon Valley. His father, Jerry Wozniak, was a graduate of the California Institute of Technology (Caltech) and an outstanding engineer who worked for the Lockheed Corporation. The elder Wozniak often brought his work home with him. Soon his son was reading adult engineering literature. This early exposure to technology enhanced his natural gift in this field. He built his own radio receiver and transmitter and earned a ham radio license, at the age of 11. Aside from his genius with amateur radios, "the Woz," as he came to be known, showed a marked ability with electronics. He would spend his time after school studying electronic trade journals. His room was filled with pictures of computers.

Despite this great interest in electronics, he also showed the normal interests of a boy in his early teens. He played on his Little League team and was fairly good at tennis. But in the eighth grade he began to show true genius. At his junior high school, he designed and built a computer that used the latest technology. It worked. Wozniak won first prize at the Bay Area Science Fair.

Wozniak's genius continued to develop at Homestead High School where he is remembered for his eccentricity as well as for his brilliance in electronics. His electronics teacher, Mr. McCollum, had a big influence on his development. They are friends to this day.

Steve graduated in the top 10 percent of his class and spent that summer trying to build a more complex computer. He and his friend Bill Fernandez would call up major electronics firms and ask them for spare (free) throwaway parts. They got the parts and built the computer, which didn't work.

WOZNIAK AND JOBS MAKE BLUE BOXES

Temporarily putting aside his interest in computers, Wozniak entered the University of Colorado in 1968. He wasn't happy. Indeed, he spent the year playing practical jokes on his dorm mates. Then he came back to Silicon Valley and enrolled in a local college, De Anza. It was during the summer after his freshman year that Bill Fernandez unwittingly made business history by introducing Wozniak to a Homestead High School senior named Steve Jobs.

Oddly enough, it was a magazine article that was to propel Wozniak in an important direction. It was an article from *Esquire* sent to him by his mother that outlined in detail a "blue box." This was an illegal electronic mechanism that could be used to make free, untraceable, and unlimited long-distance telephone calls. Wozniak decided to see if he could build one. This was probably not his mother's intent. By this time Wozniak and Jobs had become the best of friends and Jobs would often spend his free time hanging around Wozniak's room. After Wozniak built his blue box, Jobs talked him into going into the business of selling the boxes to college students.

A box cost $60 to make; the young entrepreneurs sold them wholesale for $80, making a 25 percent profit on each. After selling about 200 of these boxes—each with a note inside advertising who the builders were—the two Steves finally decided that this was much too risky a business. Two years after they began, in 1973, they closed up shop. During these two years they were becoming less and less interested in school and formal education.

Wozniak left school and tried to break into the engineering field in Silicon Valley. Finally he landed a summer job with Hewlett-Packard. There he was assigned to the advanced products division. Although he didn't have a degree and looked like a hippie, his genius with computers was instantly recognized. He moved into his own apartment in Cupertino, California.

Meanwhile, Jobs dropped out of Reed College (in Oregon), traveled to India, shaved his head, and made a determined effort to study Buddhism. The high-strung Jobs soon tired of meditating and returned to Cupertino, where he landed a job as a technician with Atari, the major manufacturer of video games. The two men again became inseparable, as Jobs introduced Wozniak to the world of video games.

THE HOMEBREW COMPUTER CLUB

Around the same time, the Homebrew Computer Club was being founded by Gordon French as a meeting place for computer enthusiasts. The first meeting of the club was held on March 5, 1975. Twenty-four people showed up. By December of that year, some 500 were attending the meetings. The Homebrew Club had an enormous influence on the development of Apple Computer. It was at these meetings that the two young would-be entrepreneurs met expert computer technicians. As a result of these encounters, many computer companies would be formed. Of the first 24 original Homebrew members, 21 became involved in forming new companies or publications, many of which are still in business. Two of the most famous are *Byte* magazine, and, of course, Apple.

Inspired by the Homebrew meetings, Wozniak became determined to build his own computer. Working after hours and relying on the study of manuals and data sheets for microprocessors as his foundation, he was able to develop a small computer. Naturally, he took it to the next Homebrew meeting. The Homebrew membership was impressed but thought the design looked unprofessional. Jobs was at this meeting. He immediately grasped the potential of Wozniak's computer.

Soon, they agreed to go into business together. But first Wozniak wanted to give his employer, Hewlett-Packard, a chance to develop his small, "personal" computer because part of his design had been developed during work time. In a now classic case of corporate misjudgment, Hewlett-Packard turned it down, not once but three times.

STARTING APPLE IN A GARAGE WITH $1,300

Now the two entrepreneurs were on their own. Jobs immediately named the company "Apple" because of a pleasant summer he'd spent picking apples after his freshman year at Reed. To get the company started, though, the partners needed investment capital. Jobs sold his Volkswagen mini-bus and Wozniak his H-P calculator. They raised about $1300, which they used to pay a friend to design a printed circuit board that cut assembly time from sixty hours to six. Next, they needed a place to work. Jobs talked his parents into letting him use their garage.

With their $1300, the garage, and Wozniak's sample computer, the two began to make sales calls. A small computer store in Mountain View sensed the hobbyists' expertise with small computers and ordered 50 of the Jobs/Wozniak models. Apple Computer was born.

The store was to pay $549 for each machine and planned to sell them for $667. They had one month to deliver. Using this order as leverage, Jobs and Wozniak next went to parts suppliers, looking for one that would give them 30-days credit. Although the two entrepreneurs looked more like hippies than businessmen, they were able to get $25,000 worth of parts on 30-days credit. They began to assemble the computers by hand in the garage. By the end of the month, they had built 100 and delivered 50 to the store in Mountain View. They paid their suppliers on the 29th day.

These first computers were called the Apple I. At first, business was slow. Only 175 computers were sold in the first year (1975-76). But it was in this first year of struggle that some of Apple's original values were formed. As Steve Jobs was to say later: "One of the things you have to remember is that we started off with a very idealistic perspective — that doing something with the highest quality, doing it right the first time, would really be cheaper than having to go back and do it again. Ideas like that."

A COMPUTER IN EVERY HOME

Jobs became convinced that Apple should try to put a computer in every home. That concept became the guiding objective of Apple. To accomplish this goal, however, they needed a better design and so Wozniak set out to build what became the Apple II. Working at night (as he was still employed at Hewlett-Packard), he spent all his free time redesigning his computer. Finally, he reached his goal. It is commonly agreed that Apple II was one of the great achievements of the computer industry.

Once Wozniak had his model, Jobs tried to round up venture capital. After exhausting his friends and family with his pleas, he finally found a major backer, Mike Markklula. Mike brought important business skills, as well as significant capital, to the operation. The original equity was set up with 26 percent each for Jobs, Wozniak, and Markklula. The remaining 22 percent was sold to other investors. When Markklula came on board, Jobs was 21 and Wozniak 25.

The company moved out of the garage and into a small facility in Cupertino. They found a high-quality promotional expert, Regis McKenna. This was 1977, Apple's first full year of operations. With manufacturing and sales in place, and some capital, Apple was ready to take off.

The Apple II made its debut at a local computer trade show. It was the first personal computer to provide color graphics and come in a light plastic case. Orders poured in and Apple was able to hire some experienced managers; some experienced, conservative investors came on the board of directors, as well, and began to turn Apple into a real business.

WOZNIAK LEAVES APPLE

In 1981, however, Wozniak was badly injured in a plane crash. He took a leave of absence from Apple and never fully returned. In an interview on his non-profit web site, www.woz.org, Wozniak says of the crash and the resultant amnesia he suffered "indirectly it was a blessing." Although he recovered from the amnesia, which was affecting his recent, but not his long-term memories, Wozniak decided to retire and devote himself to his family and non-profit pursuits. He has a tiny residual salary at Apple, "because that's where my loyalty should be forever."

Today Wozniak lives in Los Gatos, California, and is a co-owner of a server called Unuson Corp., which maintains his site as well as sites for Joan Baez, Envisioning, Inc., and other progressive artists and companies. He teaches fifth graders at the local public elementary school, and also teaches their teachers how to use technology to teach. He set the school up with Mac labs, and the library was named after him, as a result. Wozniak has donated a large portion of his wealth, over $7 million, to philanthropy — primarily through initiatives providing computers, servers, and network instruction for students and teachers. The new Children's Discovery Museum of San Jose is on 180 Woz Way.

JOBS IS KICKED OUT OF HIS OWN COMPANY

While Wozniak was recovering from his accident, Jobs was trying to turn Apple into a "grown-up company." He worked hard to convince one of the most respected executives in business, John Sculley, president of Pepsi Cola, to come on board as president and CEO. Little did Jobs know this would cost him his job!

Sculley and Jobs successfully launched the Macintosh in 1984, but by 1985 customers were complaining about the new computers' tiny memory and lack of hard drive connectivity. Jobs wanted to push to fix this problem; Sculley perceived Jobs as out of control. In May, 1985, Jobs, who had come to believe that Sculley didn't understand the computer industry, attempted to regain control of his company by scheduling a board meeting while Sculley was out of town on business. Unfortunately for Jobs, someone tipped off

Sculley and he returned to confront Jobs in the boardroom. After a heated argument between the two, the board took a vote and sided unanimously with Sculley. Jobs resigned that day.

Under Sculley's leadership, however, Apple began bleeding both money and employees. Sculley was battling for market share with Microsoft, which introduced Windows 1.0, which was very similar to the guiding interface used by the Mac. Apple lawyers were able to pressure Gates to sign a statement agreeing to not use Mac technology in Windows 1.0—but Gates wisely made sure the agreement said nothing about future versions of Windows. Apple effectively lost its exclusive rights to its interface technology, as a result.

UPS AND DOWNS FOR APPLE BRING STEVE JOBS BACK

Apple was in bad shape until it introduced the LaserWriter and PageMaker. Both the printer and the software turned the Mac into the ideal choice for inexpensive publishing. Building on this success, Apple introduced the Mac II in 1987. Apple took off once again, shipping 50,000 Macs a month.

The company faced further ups and downs with both the Microsoft-driven PC dominance and the introduction of Apple PowerBooks, which were a huge success. Sculley was replaced in 1993 with Michael Spindler, who oversaw the introduction of the PowerMac. He misjudged the computer market, however , when he pushed the inexpensive Performa over the PowerMac in the winter of 1995-96. He also licensed the Mac OS to several companies that were cloning Macs—a move that ended up creating more competition. Apple posted a $68 million loss that quarter and Spindler was replaced by Gil Amelio, former president of National Semiconductor. Amelio made widesweeping changes and did slow the losses, but he couldn't turn the company around. Apple was also hurt by the release of Windows '95, which did an even better job of mimicking the Apple interface.

In late 1996, Apple announced that it was acquiring Steve Jobs' company, NeXT. After another huge loss in 1997, Amelio resigned and Steve Jobs began to be referred to as Apple's "interim CEO." Amazingly, Jobs first step was to announce an alliance with Microsoft. In exchange for $150 million in Apple Stock, Microsoft and Apple would have a 5-year patent cross-license and would finally settle their ongoing battle over Windows technology. In addition, Microsoft announced that Office '98 would become available for the Mac.

Next Jobs tackled the problem of clones by buying out the primary cloner, Power Computing. After Apple bought out Power Computing's MacOS license and most of its engineering staff, Power went out of business and Apple took over its product support. Apple also bought out its MacOS licenses from Motorola and IBM.

JOBS TURNS APPLE AROUND

Jobs' next decisive move was his announcement on Nov. 10, 1997 that Apple would now sell computers direct via The Apple Store. Within a week it was the third largest e-commerce site on the Web. Jobs also introduced two new products, the PowerMac G3 and the PowerBook G3. For the first quarter of 1998, Jobs was able to announce a profitable first quarter, with sales of $44 million. He has kept the momentum going with the hugely popular iMac and sales figures that have pushed Apple's stock to all-time highs. In July 1999, he introduced the iBook, which has been another hot seller. Jobs is only paid $1.00 a year in salary (although he is loaded with Apple stock, of course), a bargain considering what he has accomplished since returning to the helm of Apple Computer, Inc., as its "CEO."

Meanwhile, Wozniak disputes stories of conflict between him and Jobs. On his web site, Wozniak writes: "Steve Jobs and myself are quite different. I'm quite relaxed and joking and happy working with schools and keeping some personal networks going and more. Steve is more industrious and far thinking....Partly there are misconceptions because I always tell far more of the truth than most people do, and the worst interpretations result. I and Steve are frequently misquoted deliberately and accidentally and negligently and that's how history gets written. Steve deserves recognition for what he has brought and is bringing to the world. I deserve the same, even if it's only for things I did far in the past and seemingly small. "

MORE ABOUT STEVE WOZNIAK AND STEVE JOBS

Company Web Site: www.apple.com, www.woz.org

Apple Confidential: The Real Story of Apple Computer, Inc. by Owen W. Linzmayer, No Starch Press, May 1999

Apple: The Inside Story of Intrigue, Egomania, and Business Blunders by Jim Carlton, Harperbusiness, Nov. 1998

Jerry Yang

YAHOO!

In under four years, Jerry Yang built his grad-school business idea for a Web search engine into a business worth over $30 billion. At age 32, he was worth over $3 billion, based on his stake in Yahoo!, the company he had started in 1995 with his pal David Filo. Pretty amazing for someone with no father whose mother brought him and his brother to this country when he was ten.

*"I'm having a **great** time. This is the **best** **job** I've ever had. Actually, it's the **only** job I've ever had."*

Yang was born Yang Chih-Yuan in Taipei, Taiwan, in 1967. His father, who was from mainland China, died when Yang was two. His mother moved the family to San Jose and eventually became a professor of English and drama. Yang and his brother Ken still go home on Sundays for her home cooking.

Yang was a bright, hyperactive child, especially gifted in math and science. Once in college he decided to pursue a Ph.D. in engineering at Stanford. The idea for Yahoo! was born when Yang—a still-hyperactive grad student who preferred surfing the Internet to working on his dissertation—put up a web page containing his golf scores, his name in Chinese characters, and a list of his favorite Internet sites. His friend David Filo, who was equally desperate for distraction from his dissertation, suggested that they expand Yang's list of favorite Internet sites and create a database that people could access to help navigate the Web.

Originally, the data was stored on Yang's student computer, named "Akebono," and the search engine was stored on Filo's computer, "Konishiki"—the computers having been named for two popular Hawaiian sumo wrestlers. Yang and Filo never thought Yahoo! would become big business. In fact, Yang told *Forbes* in December, 1997, "For awhile we were sitting there literally writing business plans for Internet-based businesses while on the side working on Yahoo!, thinking, 'That's never going to be a business. So we did shopping malls. We did booksellers. We actually designed a system where you could inventory and order books, similar to Amazon.com today. But at the time, we didn't realize the thing that we'd been working on for fun was going to be the one that succeeded."

It soon became clear, however, that Yang and Filo were on to something; Web surfers from all over the world were hitting their site. Filo didn't really feel comfortable having his name be part of the name for a real business, though, so the duo brainstormed until they came up with a new name. They were looking for an acronym that would start with "yet another," Yang explained in a March 3, 1999 radio interview with Motley Fools Tom and David Gardner, "because at the time, believe it or not, there were tons of directories and searches." They came up with "Yet Another Highly Officious Oracle, " or Yahoo!, for short. Considering that Filo's dad had once called them "a couple of yahoos," it seemed like a good fit.

Filo and Yang abandoned their dissertations and worked on developing customized software for Yahoo! that would help them locate, identify, and edit Web material. In early 1995 Netscape co-founder Marc Andreessen invited them to get off Stanford University's network, which they were straining, and move onto larger computers at Netscape's Mountain View, California, office. Next, venture capital firm Sequoia Capital invested $1 million. This turned out to be a very prescient investment—by the end of 1997 that stake was worth $560 million.

On Aug. 1, 1995, Yahoo! officially became a business, with Yang dubbed "Chief Yahoo!," a title he still retains on his business cards. Filo was also a Chief Yahoo!, but he changed his title to Cheap Yahoo! because he strove to make things work on off-the-shelf, no-frills PCs.

No one was more astonished by the company's rocketing success than the yahoos themselves. Yang told C/NET, "There's this huge fast-moving train called the Internet. And we're just half a mile ahead laying the tracks to make sure it doesn't go off the cliff. It's felt like that since the very beginning."

That may be, but Yang has proven to be a natural entrepreneur who jumped into the business world with both feet and discovered that he thrives on meeting with analysts and reporters alike. From the start, Yang sought to involve Yahoo! in partnerships that would help it grow from a simple portal into a new type of media company. He's developed partnerships with broadcasting companies like Fox and computer giants like Toshiba America. At breakneck pace, Yang brought himself up to speed on everything from reading annual reports to closing deals. "I've learned more than I thought I ever could have in the last two and a half years," he told Motley Fools, adding that he was never intimidated when he found himself in conference rooms with heavy hitters who were much older than he was because, "...what we do is so new. Most people are looking at us to figure out what the answer is as much as we're looking to them for help."

Today Yahoo! offers a branded network of media, commerce, and communication services to over 100 million users worldwide. Yahoo! is one of the most recognized Internet brands—a fact that draws the advertisers who provide much of the company's revenue. Yahoo! has offices in Europe, Asia Pacific, Latin American, Canada, and the U.S. and partnerships with numerous strong companies, including Fox, Healtheon, Phoenix Technologies, Autoweb.com, PageNet, Toshiba, HP, Gateway, and Japan's Softbank.

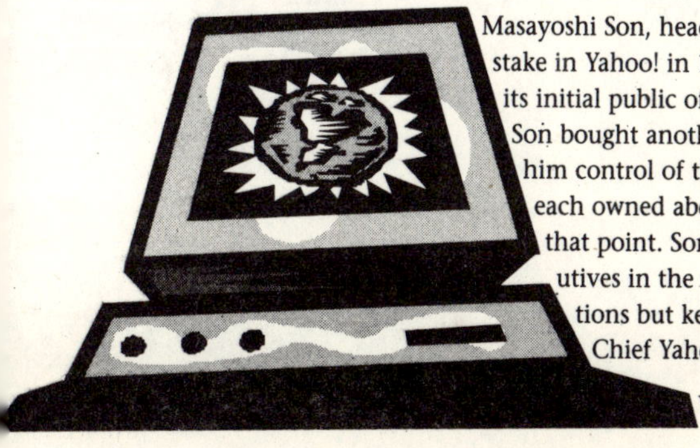

Masayoshi Son, head of Softbank, bought a 20% stake in Yahoo! in 1995, and when Yahoo! held its initial public offering a few months later Son bought another 17.025%, which gave him control of the company. Yang and Filo each owned about 12% of the company at that point. Son installed professional executives in the CEO, COO, and CFO positions but kept Yang and Filo on as Chief Yahoos.

Yang has continued to do

what he does best—create the innovative connections and partnerships that have spurred Yahoo!'s exponential growth. He likes to use a 28.8 modem to surf the Internet, so he can stay in touch with the average Yahoo! customer's experience. Meanwhile, the shier Filo has buried himself in programmer heaven. He gave up his director's title in 1996 and seems happy to focus on the technical aspects of the business and let Yang be the face of the company. Even though success has highlighted their differences, one thing remains the same: they both claim to be disinterested in the money. Neither has purchased enormous estates or fleets of Porsches and they both still pride themselves on flying coach.

Yang's latest focus is the integration of both the community and e-commerce possibilities presented by Yahoo!'s acquisitions of GeoCities, Yoyodyne Entertainment and Viaweb. Users of GeoCities, for example, can now configure their Web pages so they can sell online, for a small monthly fee. Viaweb has been turned into Yahoo! Store—it also charges a flat fee to provide everything a client could need to create an e-commerce site. Yahoo! is not only making online entrepreneurship easier, it's developing a solution to the problem of how to gather demographic information about its users. *ZDNet's* Matthew Broersme explained in his March 2, 1999 article "Yahoo! Getting Personal" that Yang believes the solution may be "permission marketing, where users exchange some personal information for a value-added service of some kind, such as a contest or for frequent-flyer points." Yoyodyne Entertainment is a permission marketing specialist.

In the Motley Fool interview, Yang described success as "personally...a dream come true and in many ways it's what America is all about: being an immigrant and leaving a place, where obviously I think nowhere else in the world could people like me do something like this."

MORE ABOUT JERRY YANG

Company Web Site: www.yahoo.com

The Quiz

"DO YOU HAVE WHAT IT TAKES?"

I hope that reading the amazing stories of the entrepreneurs in this book has inspired you to consider starting your own business. Whether you are an artist or a computer fanatic, you probably have an idea for a business you'd like to start—or you wouldn't have picked up this book. In this section, you'll learn where to find money to start your own business and you'll be guided step by step through writing a business plan that you can use to raise money.

But first, here's a fun quiz you can take to learn more about yourself and whether you have any of the characteristics it takes to be a successful entrepreneur. As you take it, think about the characteristics of the people whose lives you've read about in the previous chapters. What made them successful? Can you relate to how they handled adversity and how they responded to challenges and opportunities? Take the quiz below to see how you fare on the entrepreneurial scale. Circle the answer that best represents how you would respond.

1. You're at a party and a friend tells you that the guy in the expensive-looking suit recently invested in another friend's business. You:

(a) Race over to him, introduce yourself, and tell him every detail of your business idea while asking if he'd be interested in investing in you.

(b) Ask your friend to introduce you. When he does, hand the potential investor your business card and politely ask whether you might call on him sometime to present him with your business plan.

(c) Decide that it's probably not a good idea to bother the man at a party. After all, he's here to relax. Maybe you'll run into him again somewhere else.

2. Your boss puts you in charge of researching office supply stores and choosing the one that you think would be best for the company to use. Your response:

(a) Yes! Finally, a chance to show the boss what you're made of—plus, you'll be able to spirit a few of those supplies away for your own business.

(b) You're terrified; this is more responsibility than you really want. What if you make a mistake and cost the company a lot of money. You don't want to look bad.

(c) You're excited. This is a good opportunity to impress your boss and also learn how to compare and negotiate with suppliers—something you'll need to do for your own business.

3. You're already going to school full time when you're offered a part-time job that's in the same field as the business you want to start when you graduate next year. You:

(a) Take the job, after talking with your student advisor about how to juggle your schedule so it will fit. The experience and the contacts you'll develop will be invaluable when you start your business.

(b) Take the job. In fact, you ask for extra hours so you can finally start making some real money. Who needs sleep?

(c) Turn down the job. School is hard enough without working, too. You don't want your grades to suffer.

4. You're offered a job as a survey-taker for a marketing firm. The job pays really well but will require you to talk to a great many people. You:

(a) Take the job. You like people and this is a good way to practice getting to know what consumers want.

(b) Pass on the job; just the thought of approaching strangers makes you queasy.

(c) Take the job so you can conduct some market research of your own by also asking the people you survey what they think about your business idea.

5. Your last job paid well and was interesting but required you to put in long hours and sometimes work on the weekend. Your response:

(a) You put in the extra hours without complaint, but mainly because you felt that the rewards were worth it.

(b) You went a little overboard and worked yourself into a state of exhaustion. Moderation is not your strong suit.

(c) You quit. You are strictly a nine-to-fiver. Work is definitely not your life!

6. You are such a good guitar player that friends keep offering to pay for you to give them lessons. Your response:

(a) You spend some bucks to run a six-week ad in the local paper announcing that you are now available to teach, at the same rate that other established teachers in the area charge.

(b) You start teaching a few friends to see how it goes. You ask them what they are willing to pay and what they want to learn.

(c) You give a few friends some lessons but refuse to take any money.

7. Your best friend has started a business designing web sites. He needs help because the business is really growing. He offers to make you a partner in the business even though you are "computer illiterate." Your response:

(a) You jump in, figuring you'll learn the ropes soon enough.

(b) You ask your friend to keep the partnership offer open but first to recommend a class you can take to get your skills up to speed.

(c) You pass—you don't see how you can work in a business you know nothing about.

OK! Now you are ready to analyze your answers. Just turn the page....

ANALYSIS OF THE "DO YOU HAVE WHAT IT TAKES" QUIZ

Scoring

1. a 2 b 1 c 0
2. a 2 b 0 c 1
3. a 1 b 2 c 0
4. a 1 b 0 c 2
5. a 1 b 2 c 0
6. a 2 b 1 c 0
7. a 2 b 1 c 0

12 Points or More: You're a natural risk-taker and can handle a lot of stress. These are important characteristics for an entrepreneur to have to be successful. You are willing to work hard but have a tendency to throw caution to the wind a little too easily. Save yourself from that tendency by carefully evaluating your business (and personal!) decisions. In your enthusiasm don't forget to look at the opportunity costs of any decision you make. These are the costs of giving up the next best opportunity that you could take with your time and money. You could go to school instead of starting a business, for example. Giving up going to school and the potential rewards of that decision would be your opportunity cost.

6 to 12 Points: You strike an excellent balance between being a risk-taker and someone who carefully evaluates decisions. An entrepreneur needs to be both. You are also not overly motivated by the desire to make money, and that's good. You understand that a successful business will require hard work and some sacrifice before the rewards start rolling in. To make sure that you are applying your natural drive and discipline to the best possible business opportunity, use cost-benefit analysis to evaluate the different businesses you are interested in starting. In other words, weigh the costs (including opportunity costs!) against the benefits of starting a business.

6 Points or Fewer: You're a little cautious for an entrepreneur, but that will probably change as you learn more about how to run a business. You're concerned with financial security and may not be eager to put in the long hours required to get a business off the ground. This doesn't mean you won't succeed as an entrepreneur; just make sure that whatever business you decide to start is the business of your dreams, so that you will be motivated to make it a success. Use cost-benefit analysis to evaluate your business opportunities. Choose the one that you believe has the best shot at providing you with both the financial security and the motivation you require.

WHERE TO FIND THE MONEY TO START YOUR BUSINESS

"Sure I'd like to start a business," you might be thinking, "but where would I get the money?" That's a logical question, and lucky for you there's a logical answer: There are many sources of capital (the term businesspeople use to refer to money used for business purposes) for entrepreneurs. The catch is that to snag any of it you will have to present a coherent business plan that shows potential investors and lenders why they should give capital to you. The good news is that the next chapter shows you exactly how to write a business plan that will make them eager to do so. But first, you need to learn the difference between debt and equity financing.

DEBT VS. EQUITY FINANCING

There are two ways you can offer to compensate an investor.

1) ***Debt*** - You borrow the money and promise to pay it back over a set period of time at a set rate of interest. Corporations sell debt in the form of bonds. You could borrow money from family and friends or a bank to finance your business.

2) ***Equity*** - You give up a percentage of ownership in your business for money. The investor receives a percentage of future profits from the business based upon the percentage of ownership. Corporations sell equity in the form of stock. You cannot sell stock unless your business is incorporated, but you can sell equity. You could offer ownership and a share of your future profits in exchange for financing.

DEBT FINANCING

To finance through debt, the entrepreneur goes to a person or an institution that has money and borrows it. The entrepreneur signs a promise to repay the sum with interest. That promise is called a promissory note.

Interest is figured by multiplying the principal by the interest rate. The principal is the amount of the loan, not including interest payments. If $1,200 is borrowed at 10 percent to be paid back over one year, the interest on the loan is $1,200 x .10 or $120.

One advantage of debt is that the lender has no say in the future or direction of the business as long as the loan payments are made. Another is that the payments are predictable.

The disadvantage of debt is that if the loan payments are not made, the lender can force the business into bankruptcy to get the loan back, even if that loan is only a fraction of what the business is worth. The lender can even take the home and possessions of the owner of a sole proprietorship, or of a partner in a partnership. Yikes!

This should be carefully considered by the beginning entrepreneur because it often takes time for a new business to show a profit. The risk of debt is that failure to make loan payments can destroy the business before it gets the chance to prove itself.

EQUITY FINANCING

Equity means that, in return for money, the investor receives a percentage of ownership in the company. For the $1,200 investment we discussed above, an equity investor might request five percent ownership of the company, which would give him or her five percent of the business's profits.

If the business doesn't make profits, neither does the investor. The equity investor cannot force the business into bankruptcy to get back the original investment. If a business is forced into bankruptcy by its creditors, they get paid off first from the sale of the business assets. Equity investors have a claim on whatever is left over after debt investors have been paid.

The equity investor's risk is higher than that of the debt lender, but so is the potential for return. The equity investor could make the investment back many times over if the business prospers. He or she accepts a higher level of risk than the debt lender. The debt lender's risk of losing his or her investment is lower. So is the debt lender's return.

The advantage of equity financing is that the money doesn't have to be paid back unless the business is successful. The disadvantage is that, through giving up ownership, the entrepreneur can lose control of the business to the equity holders. That's what happened to Steve Jobs at Apple. His board, which had been largely compensated with Apple stock, was able to vote him out of the company.

THE SIX "C'S" OF BUSINESS CREDIT

Nonetheless, many businesses have been gotten off the ground with equity financing, because it can be challenging for new entrepreneurs to get bank loans. Bankers are very conservative lenders. They don't like to lend money unless they are very confident that they will get it back—after all, their jobs depend on getting it back! Bankers live and die by the Six Cs:

1. ***Collateral***—the banker wants to see you pledge property or assets against the loan that the bank can seize and sell if you stop your loan payments.

2. ***Cash Flow***—for a banker to lend you money, your business plan's projected cash flow statements must convince him or her that your business will generate enough cash to pay off the loan.

3. ***Credit History***—before a bank lends you money or a credit card company grants you a card, they will contact a credit reporting agencies (CRA) and get your credit report. These agencies, such as Trans Union and Experian, gather information given to them voluntarily by bankers, suppliers and other creditors.

4. ***Capacity***—you will also have to prove to the bank that your business's cash flow will be adequate for you to make your monthly loan payments. You will have to report your projected income and expenses so the bank can judge your "capacity," to repay the loan.

5. ***Commitment***—how much of your own money have you invested in your business? Have you gotten friends and family to invest? The banker wants to see that others are risking their money with you.

6. ***Conditions***—Finally, a bank will evaluate conditions; this is the general economic climate at the time the loan is made. If inflation is on the rise, for example, the bank may be concerned that your business earnings will not keep pace with inflation, thus reducing your capacity to repay your loan.

ESTABLISHING PERSONAL CREDIT HISTORY

If you are a small business owner looking for a loan, a bank will expect you to sign a personal guarantee that you are responsible for paying the loan. In other words, if you fail to repay, the bank can come after not only your business assets, but your personal assets, as well. The bank, therefore, will investigate your personal, as well as your business, credit history.

You may think that you have good credit because you've never borrowed money or used a credit card. Wrong. What you've got is "no credit." To establish credit you must prove that you are capable of making regular payments on a debt.

To establish credit, open a charge account, charge a few small purchases and pay for them right away. Never miss a payment or pay later than the due date.

Finally, it's wise to periodically check your credit reports on file with the credit reporting agencies every six months to make sure they are accurate. For more information, call:

**** TransUnion at 1 (800) 916-8800***

**** Experian at 1 (888) 397-3742***

**** Equifax 1 (800) 685-1111***

The CRAs do sometimes make mistakes. You can also have disputes recorded as such, not as bad credit. If you are refusing to pay for your new TV because it doesn't work, for example, you can contact the CRAs and have the debt designated "disputed," instead of "unpaid."

Keep your credit history spotless—it's virtually impossible to grow a business substantially without using some debt financing.

TIPS FOR AVOIDING A PERSONAL LOAN GUARANTEE

If you do succeed in landing a bank loan, the bank will probably want you to personally guarantee it. This means that if you default on the loan, the bank can seize not only your business but your personal assets—your house, your car, your boat (well, you'll probably be too busy running your business to use the boat much, anyway!). According to Joe Mancuso, the founder of the Center for Entrepreneurial Management, however, there are tactics you can use to avoid the sleepless nights a personal loan guarantee can cause. Mancuso's book: *How To Get A Business Loan Without Signing Your Life Away* (Prenctice Hall, 1990), has some excellent suggestions, including:

* Ask. Find out how big a company has to be before the owner doesn't have to personally guarantee a loan. Find out where your bank draws the line.

* Maybe you can't get out of the personal guarantee when you sign for the loan. But how about when you've paid off the first third? Or the first half? Ask your banker and continue to bargain once you've shown that you can pay off the loan.

* Get your banker excited about your business. Take her to lunch, tell her how you've developed a monitor that will reduce the risk of crib deaths. As Mancuso says, "help the banker be a hero."

* If you can't get off the guarantee, chip away at it in negotiations. For example, does the guarantee mean the bank can come after your personal assets right away if you miss a payment? Or does it have to sue your business first? The latter would be preferable for you.

MICROLOAN FINANCING

If you get to the point where you are negotiating a personal guarantee with a bank, you're in pretty good shape. But most young entrepreneurs will not be able to get their first shot of financing from bank. If you need a loan, however, check out the growing number of microloan programs supported by the federal government. A microloan is a loan from under $100 to $25,000 to a very small business that is given based not on credit history or collateral but on the entrepreneur's character, management ability, and business plan. The money can be used to buy machinery, furniture, inventory, and supplies for a new business but may not be used to pay existing debts.

The Small Business Administration gives local nonprofits funds to process microloan applications.

VENTURE CAPITAL

Another source of capital is investors and investment companies whose specialty is financing new, high-potential entrepreneurial companies. Because they often provide the initial equity investment to start up a business, they are called venture capitalists.

Professional venture capitalists won't usually invest in a company unless its business plan shows it is likely to generate sales of at least $25 million within five years. They typically expect to earn six times their money back over a five-year period. That works out to about a 45 percent return on investment.

Don't waste your time looking for venture capitalists, therefore, unless you are convinced that your venture will generate major returns. The ideal candidates for venture capital are businesses with financial projections that support revenue expectations of over $50 million within five years, growing at 30-50% per year, with pretax profit margins over 20%.

VENTURE CAPITALISTS WANT EQUITY

If your business plan proves that your business can generate those kinds of returns, you may be able to interest venture capitalists in your business. Venture capitalists don't lend money; they want equity in return for their capital. They are willing to take the higher risk for higher returns. Venture capitalists sometimes seek a majority interest in the business. Someone who holds a majority interest in a business owns more than fifty percent of the business and has, as a result, the final word in management decisions.

To finance the Ford Motor Company, Henry Ford gave up 75 percent of the business for $28,000 of badly needed capital. It took Ford many years to regain control of his company. Still, many small business owners turn to venture capital when they want to grow the business but can't convince banks to lend them money.

HOW VENTURE CAPITALISTS GET THEIR ROI

Venture capitalists typically reap the return on their equity investment in one of two ways:

1. The venture capitalist sells his/her percentage share of the business to another investor.

2. The venture capitalist waits until the company "goes public" (starts selling stock to the general public) and converts his/her share into stock. The stock can now be traded on the stock market.

ANGEL FINANCING

If your business is not going to pull in the kind of revenue that attracts venture capitalists, it might still be of interest to angels. Angels are private investors (nonprofessional financing sources) who are typically worth over $1 million and are interested in investing in start ups for a variety of reasons, from friendship to a desire to support entrepreneurship in a given field. Bill Gates, for example, has bankrolled several biotech startups because he's interested in the field.

If your business has good management in place and a solid business plan, you might be able to raise angel financing. Typically, startup angel financing is in the $100,000 to $500,000 range. Angels tend to seek a return of ten times their investment at the end of five years.

The idea is to get one angel in place and have that person help you find another six to eight co-investors. Your best bet may be regional venture capital networks, which often also attempt to connect entrepreneurs and angels. Regional networks can be very helpful because angels tend to invest in businesses they can visit frequently. Look for people who are interested in, or familiar with your markets and technology.

BOOTSTRAP FINANCING

Last but not least, there's always bootstrap financing. If you can't secure venture or angel financing, don't let this stop you. Many hugely successful businesses have been founded for under $10,000 by entrepreneurs who used a variety of techniques to stay afloat, including:

* *Hiring as few employees as possible. Using a temporary service for staffing needs can cut down on insurance and tax expenditures.*

* *Leasing, rather than buying, equipment.*

* *Getting suppliers to extend your credit terms so you can take longer to pay bills.*

* *Using personal savings, taking a second mortgage, arranging low-interest loans from friends and relatives.*

ACE-NET—THE ACCESS TO CAPITAL ELECTRONIC NETWORK

Finally, ACE-Net is a new resource for entrepreneurs looking for capital, advisors, and mentors. It's a secure Internet database managed by the Whittemore School of Business and Economics at the University of New Hampshire. Investors can customize the search engine to search for companies that interest them. For a $450 fee you can be listed on this national network. In addition, regional ACE-Net partners offer mentoring and advising to area entrepreneurs.

YOUR NEXT STEP: WRITING A BUSINESS PLAN THAT WILL RAISE MONEY

None of the potential capital sources described in this chapter will fork any capital over to you without seeing a thorough, detailed, convincing business plan. The next chapter is a business plan workbook that you can use to write one. Even if you plan to start your business with your own money, please take the time to go through this workbook and write yourself a business plan. It will help you figure out issues you probably aren't even aware of right now. It will also become a guide you can use as you run your business. It may even help attract more money to your business. In short, writing a business plan is a great use of your time. Plus, it's pretty fun to watch your business idea take shape on the page!

Business Plan Workbook

A STEP-BY-STEP GUIDE FROM THE NATIONAL FOUNDATION FOR TEACHING ENTREPRENEURSHIP

THE BUSINESS PLAN IS KEY TO RAISING CAPITAL

No matter whom you approach to raise money for your business, you'll need a business plan. Venture capitalists, angels, and bankers will refuse to see an entrepreneur who doesn't have a business plan. You may have a brilliant business idea, but if it is not set forth in a well-written business plan, no potential investor will be interested.

A well-written plan shows potential investors that the business owner has carefully thought through the business. All investors—bankers, friends, neighbors, or venture capitalists—crave information. The more information you offer investors about how their money will be used, the more willing they will be to invest in your business. Your plan should be so thoughtful and well written that the only question it raises in an investor's mind is: "How much can I invest?"

WRITING A BUSINESS PLAN SAVES YOU TIME AND MONEY

As you work on your business plan, problems you might not have thought of before will be uncovered. Working them out on paper will save you time and money. Before you serve your first customer, you will have answered every question you can. How much should you charge for your product or service? What exactly is your product or service? What is one unit? What are your costs? How are you going to market your product or service? How do you plan to sell it?

Such questions can quickly overwhelm you if you start a business without a plan. By the time you have used all the worksheets, however, you will have answers—and you will have a rough draft of a business plan for your own business.

Appendix I:

RESOURCES FOR ENTREPRENEURS ON- AND OFFLINE

BOOKS

Here are some of the books that entrepreneurs find helpful to have on their shelves.

Accounting...

Accounting the Easy Way, 3rd Edition, by Peter J. Eisen (New York: Barron's Educational Series, Inc., 1995).

Advertising...

Do-It-Yourself Advertising: How To Produce Great Ads, Brochures, Catalogs, Direct Mail, and Much More by Fred Hahn (John Wiley & Sons, Inc., 1993).

The Handbook of Small Business Advertising by Michael Anthony (Addison-Wesley Publishing Co., 1981).

Attitude...

Success Through a Positive Mental Attitude by W. Clement Stone (Englewood Cliffs, NJ: Prentice-Hall, 1962).

Think and Grow Rich by Napoleon Hill (New York: Harper & Row, 1989).

Think and Grow Rich by Dennis Paul Kimbro (New York: Fawcett Columbine, 1991).

Entrepreneurship...

How to Make 1000 Mistakes in Business and Still Succeed: The Small Business Owner's Guide to Crucial Decisions by Harold L. Wright (Oak Park, IL: The Wright Track, 1990).

Mancuso's Small Business Resource Guide by Joseph Mancuso (New York: Prentice-Hall Press, 1988).

101 Businesses You Can Start On The Internet by Daniel S. Janal (International Have You Got What It Takes? How To Tell If You Should Start Your Own Business by Joseph Mancuso (New York: Prentice-Hall Press, 1982).

Financing...
The Complete Guide to Money and Your Business by Robert E. Butler and Donald Rappaport (Englewood Cliffs, NJ: Prentice-Hall, Inc., 1989).

Investing..
Understanding Wall Street by Jeffrey Little (Philadelphia: Liberty Hall Press, 1991).

The Stock Market by Nancy Dunnan (Morristown, NJ: Silver Burdett Press, 1990).

Common Sense: A Simple Plan for Financial Independence (10th Revision) by Art Williams (Minneapolis: Park Lane Publishers, Inc., 1991).

Negotiation...
Field Guide to Negotiation by Gavin Kennedy (Cambridge, MA: Harvard Business School Press)

The Copyright Handbook: How To Protect and Use Written Works by Stephan Fishman (Berkeley, CA: NoLo Press, 1991).

You Can Negotiate Anything by Herb Cohen (New York: Bantam Books, 1993).

The Negotiating Game: How to Get What You Want by Chester L. Karrass (New York: Harper Business, 1992).

Win-Win Negotiation: Turning Conflict into Agreement by Fred Jandt (New York: John Wiley & Sons, Inc., 1987).

Patents and Trademarks...
Inventing and Patenting Sourcebook by Richard Levy (Detroit, MI: Gale Research, Inc., 1992).

Trademark: How to Name Your Business & Product by Kate McGrath and Stephan Elias (Berkeley, CA: NoLo Press, 1992).

Selling...

Face-to-Face Selling by Bart Breighner (Indianapolis, IN: Jist Works, Inc., 1995).

How To Sell Yourself by Joe Girard (New York: Warner Books, 1988).

Swim with the Sharks Without Being Eaten Alive by Harvey Mackay (New York: William Morrow & Co., 1988).

The Joy Of Selling by J. T. Auer (Holbrook, MA: Adams, Inc., 1991).

MAGAZINES

These magazines are well worth their subscription prices for the contacts and ideas they provide and the mistakes they can help you avoid.

Black Enterprise Magazine
130 5th Avenue, 10th Floor
New York, NY 10011-4399
(212) 242-8000
http://206.20.2.64/docs/map.html

Entrepreneur
2392 Morse Avenue
Irvine, CA 92614
(949) 261-2325
(800) 274-6229
www.entrepreneurmag.com

Fast Company
77 North Washington Street
Boston, MA 02114-1927
(800) 688-1545
www.fastcompany.com

Hispanic Magazine
331 Madison Avenue
New York, NY 10010
(212) 986-4425
www.hispanic.com

Inc.: The Magazine for Growing Companies
38 Commercial Wharf
Boston, MA 02110
(800) 842-1343
www.inc.com

WEB SITES

Here are web sites entrepreneurs need to know about—from the IRS to sources of venture and angel financing and free software.

Angelfire
www.angelfire.com, offers free space for Web sites.

Business Owner's Toolkit
www.toolkit.cch.com, loaded with tax, legal, and business info for entrepreneurs.

Electronic Commerce Guide
http://e-comm.internet.com

E-commerce News
www.internetnews.com/ec-news

Enterprise Development Web site's list of incubators
www.enterweb.org/incubator.htm

Garage.com
is a good place to hunt for both angel financing and venture capitalists: www.garage.com

InterNIC
www.internic.net, where you can register the domain name you want for your Web site.

Internal Revenue Service
www.irs.ustreas.gov./plain

National Business Incubation Association
www.nbia.org

Sell It On The Web
www.sellitontheweb.com

Shareware.com
www.shareware.com

U.S. Patent Office
http://uspto.gov

Vfinance.com
is a good place to start looking for venture capitalists www.vfinance.com

Young Entrepreneurs Network
http://www.youngandsuccessful.com

ORGANIZATIONS

The Small Business Administration (SBA) is a government agency created to support and promote entrepreneurs. The SBA offers free and inexpensive pamphlets on a variety of business subjects. Some local offices offer counseling to small business owners. Contact the SBA at:

Small Business Administration
409 Third Street, S.W.
Washington, DC 20416
(800) 827-5722
www.sbaonline.sba.gov

Small Business Answer Desk, which assists entrepreneurs with their questions and can help you locate an SBA office near you: (800) 368-5855.

The Service Core of Retired Executives (SCORE) is a group of retired businesspeople who volunteer as counselors and mentors to entrepreneurs.

Service Core of Retired Executives
26 Federal Plaza
New York, NY 10021
(212) 264-4507

National Association of Women Business Owners
1413 K St., NW, Suite 637
Washington, DC 20005
(301) 608-2590
Fax (301) 608-2596

The National Association for the Self-Employed (NASE)
1023 15th St., NW, Suite 1200
Washington, DC 20005-2600
(202) 466-2100
Fax (202) 466-2123
(800) 232-NASE

Women who need advice starting their own businesses can contact:

American Women's Economic Development Corporation (AWED)
641 Lexington Avenue, 9th Floor
New York, NY 10022
(800) 222-AWED

The National Association of Small Business Investment Companies is an association of companies that give financial assistance to small businesses. A membership directory is available for $1.00.

National Association of Small Business Investment Companies
1156 15th Street, N.W., Suite 1101
Washington, DC 20005
(202) 833-8230 Resources

Appendix II: BIBLIOGRAPHY

The following sources were used to write the twenty profiles of entrepreneurs in this book, as well as sources referenced directly in the profiles and company-produced press releases and bios.

Chapter 1: ***Jeff Bezos: Amazon.com***
Business The Amazon.Com Way: Secrets Of The World's Most Amazing Web Business By Rebecca Saunderes (Capstone Ltd., 1999)

Chapter 2: ***Richard Branson: Virgin Group Ltd.***
Richard Branson: The Authorized Biography by Mick Brown Trafalgar Square, 1998

Forbes interview with Branson, 1997

Chapter 3: ***Thomas Burrell***
Black Journalism Review, Oct. 24, 1999

Chapter 4: ***Candice Carpenter: I-Village***
(All sources referenced in profile)

Chapter 5: ***Debbi Fields: Mrs. Fields' Cookies***
One Smart Cookie by Debbi Fields (out of print)

Chapter 6: ***Henry Ford: Ford Motor Company***
Wheels Of Time: A Biography Of Henry Ford by Catherine Grouley Millbrook, 1997

Chapter 7: ***Bill Gates: Microsoft, Inc.***
The Road Ahead by Bill Gates, Penguin, 1995

Business @ the Speed of Thought by Bill Gates, Warner Books, 1999

Gates: How Microsoft's Mogul Reinvented An Industry—And Made Himself The Richest Man In America by Stephan Manes and Paul Andrews, Touchstone, 1994

Chapter 8: ***King C. Gillette***
King C. Gillette, The Man and His Wonderful Shaving Device
by Russell B. Adams (out of print)

Chapter 9: ***Berry Gordy: Motown***
The Songs of Berry Gordy; The Music, The Magic, The Memories of Motown
by Jeanette Delissa, 1995

Chapter 10: ***John Johnson***
Succeeding Against The Odds by John H. Johnson,
Amisted Press, 1993

Chapter 11: ***Robert Johnson: BET***

Chapter 12: ***Ray Kroc: McDonald's***
Grinding It Out: The Making of McDonald's by Ray Kroc,
St. Martin's Press, 1990

McDonald's: Behind The Arches by John Love, Bantam, 1995

Chapter 13: ***Spike Lee: 40 Acres and a Mule***
Spike Lee: By Any Means Necessary by Jim Haskins, Walker and Co., 1997

Best Seat In The House: A Basketball Memoir by Spike Lee, Ralph Wiley,
Three Rivers, 1998

Chapter 14: ***Anita Roddick: The Body Shop, Inc.***
Anita: The Woman Behind The Body Shop by Jules Older,
Charlesbridge Publishing, 1998

Body and Soul: Profits With Principles by Anita Roddick,
Russell Miller (out of print)

Chapter 15: ***Russell Simmons: Def Jam***
(All sources referenced in profile)

Chapter 16: ***Madame C.J. Walker***
Madame C.J. Walker: Cosmetics Tycoon by A'Lelia P. Bundles
(Walker's great-great-granddaughter), Matilda Publications, New York, 1983

Madame C.J. Walker by Cookie Lommel, Holloway House Publishing, 1993.

Chapter 17: ***Sam Walton: Wal-Mart***

Sam Walton: Made In America: My Story by Sam Walton, John Huey, Bantam Books, 1993

Wal-Mart: A History of Sam Walton's Retail Phenomenon, Twayne Publishing, 1997

Chapter 18: ***Oprah Winfrey: Harpo Productions***

Oprah by Judeth Mahoney Pasternak, Metro Books, 1999

The Uncommon Wisdom of Oprah Winfrey: A Portrait In Her Own Words by Oprah Winfrey and Bill Adler (editor), Citadel Publishing, 1999.

Chapter 19: ***Steve Wozniak and Steve Jobs: Apple Computers***

Apple Confidential: The Real Story of Apple Computer, Inc. by Owen W. Linzmayer, No Starch Press, 1999

Apple: The Inside Story of Intrigue, Egomania, and Business Blunders by Jim Carlton, HarperBusiness, 1998

Chapter 20: ***Jerry Yang: Yahoo!***

(All sources referenced in profile)